THE COLLECT[...]
15 WOMEN IN MINISTRY

The PreacHER IN HER
LIVING
The Call

DR. JOE L. STEVENSON

Copyright @ 2024 Dr. Joe L. Stevenson
ISBN: 979-8-9904970-6-1
All rights reserved.

Author owns complete rights to this book and may be contracted in regards to distribution. Printed in the United States of America.

Library of Congress Cataloging-in-Publication Data

The copyright laws of the United States of America protect this book.
No part of this publication may be reproduced or stored in a retrieval system for commercial gain or profit.

No part of this publication may be stored electronically or otherwise transmitted in any form or by any means (electronic, photocopy, recording) without written permission of the author except as provided by USA copyright law.

The Holy Bible, King James Version (KJV) . Amplified (AMP) Copyright © 1954, 1958, 1962, 1964, 1965, 1987 by The Lockman Foundation

shero Publishing
SHEROPUBLISHING.COM

Editing: SynergyEd Consulting/ synergyedconsulting.com
Graphics & Cover Design: Greenlight Creations Graphics Designs
glightcreations.com/ glightcreations@gmail.com

Be it advised that all information within this literary work, The PreacHER in Her, has been acknowledged to be the truthful accounts of each co-author. The co-authors are responsible for their contributions and chapter accuracy and hold SHERO Publishing harmless for any legal action arising as a result of their participation in this publication.

The PreacHER in Her: Living the Call is a must-read for everyone in Leadership and Followship! These stories will enlighten, encourage, and inform you that the Walk and Work of the Sister Preacher is important and necessary. Kudos to Bishop Stevenson for gathering these awesome Women of God to share their journeys.

~**Pastor Mark T. Gibson, D.Min**
Redeeming Love Missionary Baptist Church Raleigh, NC

The PreacHER in HER: Living the Call is the exact book that every little girl in churches around the world should be given. This is the exact book every woman who has entered Seminary should read before they take their first course. This is the EXACT book I wish someone had given me as I experienced the contradiction of what God was saying in my heart and what the preacher was saying in his sermons. The stories of each woman and her lived experiences will touch each heart and change the trajectory of covert and painful patriarchy in Christendom and beyond. Collectively, these voices give testimony to the connection between God's calling and female resilience.

Dr. Joe Stevenson's own personal evolution sets him apart from the traditions of old within our denominations and churches that injured and stymied women from assuming their rightful placement in the Lord's Church and Kingdom ministry. Now, this masterpiece anthology lifts his support of God's call on women and places his voice as a marker for years to come. I hope many male pastors, bishops, and seminarians will experience the same evolution as they read this magnificent book.

~**Bishop Corletta J. Vaughn, Ph.D.**
Living with the Advantage, Teach Your Daughters to Fly, Dream Again.
Assistant Professor of Leadership and Pneumatological Studies; Ecumenical Theological Seminary, Detroit, MI; Senior Pastor Holy Ghost Cathedral; and Presiding Prelate of Go Tell It Ministry, Worldwide.

The PreacHER in Her: Living the Call birthed from the editor's conversion to critique systematic oppression against women preachers, centers, critiques, and celebrates fifteen creative, committed, consecrated preachers who have staked their claims and lived out God's commission on their lives. With creative compassion, they tell their raw stories, and speak of the challenges and complicated behaviors, as they "walk in expectation and not anticipation." This book is a must-read for those curious about women preachers' experiences toward seeing the profound presence and work of God in their lives.

~**Rev. Cheryl A. Kirk-Duggan, Ph.D.**
Professor (Retired), Scholar, Clergy, Author, and Performer

Table of Contents

Dedication 6
Preface 7

Ministry Journeys

Chapter 1	Rev. Dr. Tiffany Bennett-Cornelous	Don't "Just" Me!	12
Chapter 2	Rev. Dr. Betty J. Erwin	My Journey: Embracing God's Calling	26
Chapter 3	Rev. Chanetta Lytello-Farmer	Fit for Service: God Called Me & That's Enough!	38
Chapter 4	Rev. Dr. Katrina Futrell	On Eagle's Wings	50
Chapter 5	Rev. Dr. Towanda Garner	My Help Comes from the Lord: The Strength Within	62
Chapter 6	Rev. Nichole Lynnese Harris Glover	The "S" on My Chest	74
Chapter 7	Rev. Dr. Mary McDougal-Heggie	Trust the Process	90
Chapter 8	Rev. Dr. Pamela C. Holder	From the Pit to the Pulpit	102
Chapter 9	Rev. Marlo McCloud	Challenges, Instructions & Guidance	114
Chapter 10	Rev. Yolande Murphy	The Product, The Pieces and The Platform	128
Chapter 11	Rev. Dr. Monica Redmond	I'm Preaching with a Limp	140
Chapter 12	Rev. Toshiba Rice	Handpicked for the Harvest	154
Chapter 13	Rev. Dr. Shalonda Schoonmaker	Caged Bird Singing	166
Chapter 14	Rev. Kimberly Waldon	Finally Revealed... Journeys of Grace	178
Chapter 15	Rev. Dr. Karen Wicker	Invited to the Party, But No One Asked Me to Dance!	190
Host Bio	Rev. Dr. Joe L. Stevenson		206

Dedication

The PreacHER in Her: Living the Call, a book compilation of women pastors and preachers, is dedicated to all preaching/ministering women. The stories of the 15 women preachers in this book compilation are stories of the sister preachers' perseverance and grace. Though painful at times, their ministry pursuit and ministry progress are a testimony of the ***PreacHER.*** The stories of the sister preachers are stories of triumph amid traditional trauma, patriarchal suppression, misogyny, and untold troubling situations. It is our prayer that the stories of these preaching women will inspire prayer and advocacy for all preaching women living the call. These stories are not written to generate pity for the authors. For they each are sustained by the grace of their call and their highly competent preaching gifts. Pity is not their story. These preaching gifts are living the call and not the complaints. Their preaching heralds the promises of God, not the problems of cultural constraints.

This book is dedicated to my wife, Brenda Marie, the pastor's wife, (a story yet to be told) who encouraged this compilation and our daughters, Makiea and Briona. This book is also dedicated to my mother, Rena Stevenson, grandmothers: Lydia Stevenson and Iola Keel, mother-in-love, Hattie Ray Smith, and sister, Pocahontas Logan; all at rest from their labor. I watched their journeys as they served the Body of Christ. They died in the faith with ministry scars as testimony of their labor. Lastly, this book is dedicated to my three sisters; Doris, Debra, and Brenda, all of which continue to live out their life purpose and callings.

Rev. Dr. Joe L. Stevenson
Book Compilation Visionary

Preface

Some women wait for something to change, and nothing changes, so they change themselves. Audre Lourde

This book compilation grew out of my personal transformation and evolution regarding women preachers. At my core, I have always possessed a strong affinity for my sister preacher. However, early in my ministry my mind and actions were trapped by tradition and held hostage by xenophobic and misogynistic suppression. Very early in my ministry, I relegated the sister preacher to the main floor and not to the pulpit. Like many, I too, was guilty of wandering in my thoughts as the sister preached. In my mind, this was not done to hurt the sister preacher, but it did. This was not done out of flagrant disregard of her call. As I am now in a different place and looking back, I can say the normalization, the hurt that occurred was indeed flagrant disregard of her call and identity. Those times I did not advocate for the sister preacher; I was complicit. At my core, I believed differently, but I did little to challenge the patriarchal system that had gripped the culture of the church community in which I was involved.

Then, the Holy Spirit called me to the carpet. My verbose rhetoric, disapproval, and disagreement had a day of reckoning. This glorious encounter with the Holy Spirit gave me a new perspective. Upon a deeper reflection of the Pauline epistle to the church at Corinth- I could no longer ignore, *"Therefore, since through God's mercy we have this ministry, we do not lose heart"* (2 Corinthians 4:1 NIV)- my disposition was disrupted. Nor could I escape the message in the scripture- *"All this is from God, who reconciled us to himself through Christ and gave us the ministry of reconciliation"* (2 Corinthians 5:18).

It's through God's mercy that I (we) have this ministry. The arrogance of any disposition that refused to come in alignment with the biblical truth *that it's through God's mercy that we have this ministry.* Not only that, but <u>we</u> have the Ministry of Reconciliation. The preaching of the gospel is a shared grace. Walking in this new revelation, the Holy Spirit set me on the path of advocacy.

The first sister preacher I licensed and ordained was not without great challenge. I prepared her for ordination and called for the Moderator of the district association to assemble an ordination council to ordain this sister. All of this was done in violation of the church's constitution which prohibited a woman from preaching in the pulpit. I didn't have time to go through the long and arduous process of revising the church's constitution. A preacher had come forth and needed my pastoral advocacy. I put my pastorate on the line because we have the Ministry of Reconciliation. The day came when I, along with the church, and associate preachers, two of which were women, were invited to preach at another church. The pastor met at the base of the pulpit; whispering in my ear, he said to me, "Dr., you know women aren't allowed in the pulpit here." My response was, "Pastor, you invited the church and me, and these sisters are preachers in our church. We certainly don't want to disrupt your order, but if they cannot join me as per your invitation, we will leave." He relaxed his position, and the sister preachers joined me in the pulpit. Both churches rejoiced because this was the first time women preachers sat in that pulpit. It was also the last time I was invited to that church. A few years later that church permanently closed.

The collection of stories, in this book, are the stories of 15 dynamic Sister Preachers who are Living the Call. They are courageous in Christ. Their stories are compelling. The system hasn't changed, the Sister Preachers in this book changed. They decided to live the call. The Sister Preachers living the call deserve access and acceptance. They deserve more than our "Amen"; they require our advocacy. Especially, the sister preachers still struggling to live the call as the women in this book compilation are doing. May their stories lift you up so you too can encourage, embrace, and experience *"The PreacHER in Her: Living the Call."*

THE AUTHORS:

Rev. Dr. Tiffany Bennett-Cornelous
Rev. Dr. Betty J. Erwin
Rev. Chanetta Lytello-Farmer
Rev. Dr. Katrina Futrell
Rev. Dr. Towanda C. Garner
Rev. Nichole L. Harris Glover
Rev. Dr. Mary McDougal-Heggie
Dr. Pamela C. Holder
Rev. Marlo McCloud
Rev. Yolande Murphy
Rev. Dr. Monica D. Redmond
Rev. Toshiba Rice
Rev. Dr. Shalonda Schoonmaker
Rev. Kimberly Waldon
Rev. Dr. Karen Moore Wicker

**THE COLLECTIVE JOURNEYS OF
15 WOMEN IN MINISTRY**

The PreacHER IN HER Living The Call

Chapter 1

Rev. Dr. Tiffany Bennett-Cornelous

Rev. Dr. Tiffany Bennett-Cornelous

Reverend Dr. Tiffany Benisha Bennett-Cornelous is a tither, preacher, singer, musician, professor, and community and organizational leader. The Cross, South Carolina, native and great-granddaughter of a pastor, Rev. Louis Wilson, relocated to Raleigh, North Carolina, with an academic scholarship to attend Shaw University, the oldest historically black college/university in the South.

In 1998, Rev. Dr. Bennett-Cornelous completed undergraduate coursework and earned a Bachelor of Science Degree in Computer Science. She worked as a software engineer, interning while in college, and was offered a full-time position upon graduation. She also earned the professional distinction of Master of Divinity from Shaw University Divinity School in 2014. Dr. Bennett-Cornelous successfully defended her dissertation entitled, "Parishioners' Lived Experiences of Female Leaders in a Predominantly African American Nondenominational Church", September 6, 2018. In addition, she earned a Doctor of Philosophy degree in organizational leadership.

At an early age, Rev. Dr. Bennett-Cornelous developed an affinity for musicality, inspired by her father, Benjamin Bennett. She began honing skills as a singer and organist at Antioch Holiness Church located in her hometown. As her skills progressed, she formally studied music appreciation and theory. She has contributed to numerous musical productions. She was featured on Coco McMillan's recording, "Wonderful," appeared on television programs: *Bobby Jones Presents* and *Spiritual Awakening* with Nat Gaiter & Company, and served as a background vocalist and organist for other artists, including providing vocal support for Elder Peggy Britt at the Hampton Ministers' Conferences since 2016. Dr. Bennett-Cornelous served as organist and Minister of Music in three churches. She has also served as the Assistant

Academic Dean, Director of Continuing Education, and Interim Director of a Master of Arts program at two seminaries.

In March 2012, she was licensed to preach and was ordained in January 2015, both while serving at Brighter Hope Christian Fellowship under the pastoral leadership of Bishop Blanzie Williams, Jr., Rev. Dr. Bennett-Cornelous currently serves as the Pastor of Worship, Arts & Media at Macedonia New Life Church under the leadership of her senior Pastor and Bishop-elect, The Reverend Dr. Joe L. Stevenson. Rev. Dr. Bennett-Cornelous is the Director of Music for the General Baptist State Convention of North Carolina, Inc.; Dean of the Heritage School of Biblical & Theological Studies, which is her church's leadership training academy; and Adjunct Professor of Practical Ministry at Shaw University Divinity School. She was the first professor to teach a course in the Black Church Leadership Academy at Shaw University in Introduction to Church Worship and created the first Faith-Based Nonprofit Organizational Leadership course for the Divinity School. She is the first to serve as a Principal Project/Program Manager in Faith-Based Initiatives at Blue Cross NC, where she travels the state learning from faith leaders about their congregations and community work, and she researches ways for the organization to align with the local faith community.

Rev. Dr. Bennett-Cornelous uses her knowledge, skills, and abilities to serve in various voluntary capacities for professional, civic, and social organizations. She served as a clinician, staff musician, singer, and director of music for the Shaw University Divinity School Alexander/Pegues Ministers' Conference and music coordinator and worship leader for the Shaw University Divinity School chapel services under the leadership of Dr. Joe L. Stevenson. Rev. Dr. Bennett-Cornelous was the music coordinator for the City of Raleigh Human Relations Commission, Raleigh-Apex NAACP, and North Carolina NAACP; was the first to serve as Vice President of Divinity Concerns for the National Alumni Association of Shaw University; is First-Vice President for the Shaw University Divinity School National Alumni Association, a member of Alpha Kappa Alpha Sorority, Incorporated, and the recipient of the 2024 Gus Witherspoon Award in Religion.

Rev. Dr. Bennett-Cornelous is married to her best friend and fellow musician, Ronald Lee Cornelous. For 18 years, they have jointly proclaimed the Gospel of Jesus Christ and the redeeming love of God. The quote "God hand-picked me to be a vessel of melodies for Him. I was made to worship Him. I told His story through music and now I continue to tell His story through the preached Word. I worship Him for who He is. I praise Him for what He's done, is doing, and will do" best reflects her spiritual mantra. Her life scripture is "Do not be anxious about anything, but in everything by prayer and supplication with thanksgiving let your requests be made known to God. And the peace of God, which surpasses all understanding, will guard your hearts and your minds in Christ Jesus" (Philippians 4:6-7).

To connect with Rev. Dr. Tiffany Bennett-Cornelous
Facebook: @ DrTiffany B. Bennett-Cornelous
Instagram: drtbcornelous
Email: DrTBCornelous@gmail.com

Don't "Just" Me!

Suppose a man comes into your meeting wearing a gold ring and fine clothes, and a poor man in filthy old clothes also comes in. ³ If you show special attention to the man wearing fine clothes and say, "Here's a good seat for you," but say to the poor man, "You stand there" or "Sit on the floor by my feet," ⁴ have you not discriminated among yourselves and become judges with evil thoughts? James 2:2-4

I wrote and delivered a sermon entitled, *"Don't Just Me"*[1] (Bennett-Cornelous, Don't Just Me, 2015) at my alma mater for a chapel service. The Lord gave me the inspiration from a job experience. At that time, I was responsible for moving and setting up all technical equipment for my department staff. I saved my office for last, right next to my director. I remember sitting in my office chair, looking out the window, and sighing because it had been long days of planning to make sure the move was seamless.

Upon returning from lunch, I stepped into my office—all of my equipment and furniture —gone! I stepped back into the hall to check that I had come to the right area. I was at the right office, but there were storage boxes stacked in there. My director called me to her office and explained that she received notice from two levels above her that I had to be moved—that I was "just" an office manager and did not deserve that much square footage. I was offered a cubby in the customer service area (which was kept dark as an accommodation for an employee) or a space on the other side of the building. Neither would satisfy

---

[1] Tiffany Bennett-Cornelous, "Don't Just Me," 2015, Shaw University Divinity School, Raleigh, NC, sermon.

me. In the meantime, remember that my equipment and furniture had already been moved. Where, might you ask? To the basement of the building. I was even told that I should say, "thank you" to the person who wiped the dust off the desk in the new area because it was filthy. I did not.

That wasn't my first time being "justed", but it was the first time anyone ever said it, which illumined all of my experiences and made them live in "just" moments.

You're Just a...

Being "justed" is a form of ostracization and marginalization. To be marginalized is to be assigned a lesser value or treated as insignificant. To be marginalized means you do not matter as much. To be ostracized is to be excluded from a group or activity. To be ostracized means you do not matter at all. In the book of James, chapter 2, James warns against partiality, and he lets you know that faith without works is dead. He warns against favoritism, against judging people for how they appear on the outside by saving a good seat for them and separating those from you who are not meeting your standards. Who told you that who you are and what you have sets the bar for separating groups of people? Don't *just* me!

Justed in Ministry.

In a previous ministry assignment, I was denied a promotion to a position that was vacant—not because I am a woman, but because I am not a man. "I think a man would do better" was what I was told. The rationale? Because most of the ministry consisted of women and a man could get them to comply more than a woman. I stayed in my role for one more year and then I resigned to serve in that leadership role at another church. It was disheartening and disappointing because I had done so much to prepare to be in that role, just to be told to my face that a man would do better. Unfortunately, I am not the only one who has ever experienced this disappointment. Cecelia E. Greene Barr described a similar incident in her life when she was made aware of an opportunity in full-time ministry.² Barr's "no" to her inquiry was met with the committee not being ready to fill the position AND that no additional inquiry on her part was necessary. She later discovered that the committee was holding out for a male candidate. She was lied to. At least my "no" was undergirded by their truth from their perspective—that a man would do better.

In another previous ministry assignment, a choir member told me that I was *just* the musician. This older woman did not believe that I should have any leadership authority as Minister of Music for the church. She did not believe that I should express any directives to the choir and musicians and therefore, should have had no authority to speak in other settings in the church ministry. I later learned that she believed the pastor was *just* a man so then she was justified in her consistency at least, however harmful her approach and perception.

I lead the music ministry of my church; therefore, I travel when my Pastor is called to preach. As I walk in accompanying the singers of my church, I am often viewed as the choral director. As I move to the organ or keyboard, in most cases, the gentleman already occupying the instrument looks at me in either disbelief or amazement—a woman? YES...a woman! Side note: There have been countless times when a guest preacher at my church would say in the microphone that they need a little more volume from the mic or in the monitors, "sound man". The leader of the audio ministry is a woman. There are so many assumptions in the church.

Justed in the Preparation.

At the time I accepted the call to preach, I was advised by a few men to *just* go to a local studies program, but I knew that while ministry is not a competition to me, to my male counterparts, it was and is. A few women in my life whom I highly respected and often leaned on for advice asked me why I

---

² Cecelia E. Greene Barr, "This is My Story," ed. C.J. LaRue (Louisville: Westminster John Knox Press, 2005), pg #s. (ex: 177-78)

felt the need to go back to school for a Ph.D. "You have enough [education] to do what you're doing now," was what I was told. I was also admonished in my desire for a Ph.D. and instead to obtain a Doctor of Ministry degree. Therefore, if I was going to have any respect among those who would be considered my peers, I chose to attend a brick-and-mortar institution and excel. The call on my life was to preach and the first step is the call to prepare (I learned that from my former pastor). I was preparing to walk in the call, not preparing for the constant and consistent marginalization, ostracization, and demeaning.

Justed from Leadership.

Referring to me on purpose as "Sister Tiffany" and calling my male counterpart, one of whom has no credentials, "Doctor" is disheartening, disappointing, rude, short-sided, and cowardly. After attending my doctoral graduation, my father told me to demand that people call me what I have earned. While I was in the doctoral program, every time I talked to my father, I was either reading or writing. He could attest to the time invested. My father was so amazed to see all the doctoral graduates walk across the stage. The day was not about his daughter, the graduate. It was about his daughter, the Doctor— The Reverend Doctor. I am called to preach and was trusted in the process to be ordained. I earned that Ph.D. and every other academic distinction.

The Dark Side of Grace

During our sessions preparing for this project, I shared with the co-authors that often, women are expected to be gentle in their response to trauma. I encouraged them to peel back the layers and be settled in the fact that situations may not have been resolved or ended positively. How many of these scriptures have we heard? "A gentle answer turns away wrath, but a harsh word stirs up anger" (Prov 15:1, NIV). From the Sermon on the Mount, people have extracted "turn the other cheek" (Matt 5:38-48). I did not always have the desire to be kind or graceful in my response to marginalization [trauma]. Perpetually being kind in those moments made me feel that the marginalization would never stop—as if I affirmed the "advice". As much as I wanted to give grace because of expectation, how I was raised, or because of what the Bible says I should do—the bright side—there was a dark side of that grace. Sometimes, "Some stuff ain't a revelation, it's a **reminder.**"[3] When people are intentionally disrespectful, it is a reminder that overcoming is still on its journey.

Overcoming marginalization may not ever see the light of day. It constantly happens. I am able to speak to it and call it out, but I still walk a fine line *when I choose to* speak to it or call it out. I analyze who is saying it and the environment because I am cognizant of who I am and in what role I may be operating at the time. I still need to be happy with myself when it is all over.

Apologetically Submissive

At some point, I believed that I should approach simple conversations in a way that would not be perceived as aggressive, yet assertive. For so many years, I was conditioned to either agree, even if I disagreed, in order to be a team player or disagree with some sort of preamble. For example, "I don't mean to be rude, but…" or "In my opinion…" and after giving my opinion, saying, "It's just my opinion." I did not want to be misunderstood or mischaracterized. I did not want to be labeled *the angry black woman*. If I was asked a question, did I not deserve to speak the truth? Operating with this approach, I was mostly silent on matters in all areas of my life for the sake of avoiding the appearance of being [always] contrary. I was not trying to please everyone. In corporate America, I was trying to keep my job. In ministry, I was trying to be obedient. In my personal life, I was trying to be accommodating. I was trying to thrive.

---

[3] Marcus Cosby, June 2022, Hampton, VA, sermon.

Ask any woman—most of us know what it's like to be misheard, mischaracterized, or misrepresented by family, friends, or strangers. FEW of us feel deeply known and understood all the time. Worse, many of us have endured long, painful seasons of misunderstanding in which the people around us have questioned—or worse, judged—our motives and actions. We have asked ourselves, "How do I correct these misperceptions? Do I try to defend myself—or does that only make me look guilty? How can I recover my joy even if someone believes something about me that isn't true?"[4]

Too many times have I expended energy being sensitive to what others may think about me. I have refrained from doing and saying many things because I did not want my witness of Christ to be mischaracterized. There are some things I will not do, but it is because of my own conviction and not of concern for what other people may think. The mischaracterization, mishearing, and misrepresentation is on the one committing the act. I realized that I needed to stand and be intentional in the exactness of my speech, be clear in my actions, and illumine when someone else has decided to unwarily stand in the gap for me.

Before I answered the call to preach, I served in ministry as a singer and musician. I still do, but most people know me as the singer and musician. Had it not been for social media, I am not certain anyone would know that I preach. I never thought I would have to broadcast it—definitely not through social media to gain invitations. It seemed to be boasting or bragging in a negative way and I have chosen to wait on God. I don't blame people for this at all. For 31 years, I was a singer and musician. At this point that is over 60% of my life. I cannot blame people for what they do not know about me. God has been faithful in placing me in the right place at the right time. I can say firmly that I am not *just* a singer or musician. I proclaim the Word of God through the preached Word.

---

[4] Mary DeMuth, *The Most Misunderstood Women of the Bible: What Their Stories Teach Us about Thriving* (Washington, D.C.: Salem Books, 2022).

Walk in Expectation, Not Anticipation

I have and still do have advocates, allies, and affirming people in my life. I question why people have to be in these categories at all. When I shared my belief in the call on my life to preach, my Pastor at that time took much of his time to help me understand the "why". He nurtured the call and encouraged me to prepare through education. He gave me choices to consider, and I chose a formal seminary experience. He had no problem elevating women, and the pulpit was no stranger to seeing women lead. What I like about him is that he never made it a point to place a woman in the forefront for the sake of her being a woman. I observed him teaching all the associate ministers and nurturing our gifts. He taught "operating in your gift" and he operated as Pastor by assigning according to gifts—gender unrelated.

I remember one year being at the Hampton Ministers' Conference in Hampton, Virginia. Sitting on the front row while witnessing Pastor Jamal Bryant wreck the house, I heard the Spirit of the Lord, "How did *she* get on stage?" *She* was me and the Holy Spirit was telling me right then what my peers were saying. That morning was my first time on the main stage providing vocal support to Elder Peggy Britt. It was monumental because I watched her over the years, ministering music through her bout with cancer. Earlier that year, she was at a church in town where my Pastor was preaching. My Pastor stood to give preliminaries before his sermon, and he introduced Elder Peggy Britt to me from the pulpit. I melted. My Pastor knew how much I loved her ministry, and he took a small moment to make a monumental difference. After the service, she gave me her number and asked if I would be in Hampton. When we spoke some weeks later, she asked me to accompany her on stage for the morning worship services. A dream became a reality and it lasted for seven years. God made room and opportunity for the gift through an advocate.

It wasn't until I was asked to serve in music ministry for a service, I never expected to serve that my Pastor, the visionary for this book compilation, said, "Always walk in expectation and not anticipation." This statement has stuck with me since then, and now I walk in expectation, knowing that God makes room for the gift every single time. Sometimes, I feel forgotten, but I keep moving. Sometimes, I feel taken for granted, but I keep pressing. And then...a call out of the blue or an opportunity to serve lets me know I am not forgotten or taken for granted...just delayed communication for God's time.

Oh, the things I have learned! I have hindsight, insight, and now foresight because of these lessons:

1. I did not understand God's character until God shut doors in my face.

2. The Reverend Dr. Gina Stewart, in her sermon at the National Baptist Convention, Inc. extended the invitation to "be like Claudia, to be unapologetic, to be unashamed, to be courageous, to be undaunting ...to speak up for Jesus."[5] Whenever I have the opportunity, I'll *just* preach Jesus!

3. "Seminary didn't prepare me for a lot of things as Pastor. Some things, I had to wait on the cemetery to do."[6] I. I might be *justed* plenty more times until Christ returns. In the meantime, I will watch and wait as God moves the barriers.

4. You can't have a message in this *mess*age without some mess."[7] My testimony will come from this mess of marginalization.

5. Life can only be lived forward but understood. backwards.

---

[5] Gina Stewart, "What We Gone Do with Jesus of Nazareth" January 2024, National Baptist Joint Board Session, Memphis, TN, sermon.
[6] Rev. Dr. Joe L. Stevenson, "Let's Stay Together" March 10, 2024, New Jerusalem Community Church, Durham, NC, sermon.
[7] Adrian D. Reid, n.d., sermon.

How can I ask God for stability when I do not have a standard of integrity? I have to have standards. When someone tells me my standards are too high, I tell them their expectations are too low. You don't want anything if mediocre is good enough. I learned that from my mother. When your standard is based in excellence to please God, then you tend to live in expectation of God and God's blessing. How can we ask for unity but don't accept God's standards for equality? There are some things that need to be met with a resounding, THAT STOPS HERE. We have allowed our sociological culture to inform our theological ignorance. Women can do more than clean Communion trays!

I cannot help anyone understand the struggle of a woman preacher through the eyes of one with a protruding extremity. The *Strong Black Woman*[8] may be a threat to men and women everywhere, but this is who I am. I resonate that I may have to cross "the fine line from discipleship to martyrdom."[9] She posited that many women have had to do this and some without the support or affirmation from people for such a long time. My research revealed of a nondenominational church that they were not afraid of having a woman as pastor. Despite the stereotypes, there was clear evidence that their readiness had everything to do with the candidate's qualifications.[10] I have learned that I can only stand on the Word of God and declare the name of Jesus as the standard. God has been and is working behind the scenes in my face! We are still becoming, as former FLOTUS Michelle Obama said. Isn't that a shame?

---

[8] Chanequa Walker-Barnes, *Too Heavy a Yoke* (Eugene: Wipf and Stock Publishers, 2014).

[9] Ibid.

[10] Tiffany Bennett-Cornelous, "Parishioners' Lived Experiences of Female Leaders in a Predominantly African American Non-denominational Church" (Dissertation, The Chicago School of Professional Psychology, 2018), Proquest.

Bibliography

Barr, Cecelia E. Greene. "This is My Story," ed. C.J. LaRue (Louisville: Westminster John Knox Press, 2005).

Bennett-Cornelous, Tiffany. "Don't Just Me" 2015, Shaw University Divinity School, Raleigh, NC, sermon.

Bennett-Cornelous, Tiffany. "Parishioners' Lived Experiences of Female Leaders in a Predominantly African American Non-denominational Church" (Doctoral dissertation, The Chicago School of Professional Psychology, 2018), Proquest.

Cosby, Marcus. June 2022, Hampton, VA, sermon.

DeMuth, Mary. *The Most Misunderstood Women of the Bible: What Their Stories Teach Us about Thriving* (Washington, D.C.: Salem Books, 2022).

Reid, Adrian D., n.d., sermon.

Stevenson, Rev. Dr. Joe L. "Let's Stay Together" March 10, 2024, New Jerusalem Community Church, Durham, NC, sermon.

Stewart, Gina. "What We Gone Do with Jesus of Nazareth" January 2024, National Baptist Joint Board Session, Memphis, TN, sermon.

Walker-Barnes, Chanequa. *Too Heavy a Yoke* (Eugene: Wipf and Stock Publishers, 2014).

Chapter 2

Dr. Betty J. Erwin

Dr. Betty J. Erwin

Dr. Betty J. Erwin began her ministry in 1989 and was ordained as a minister in 1993. She served as the lead associate minister at Gethsemane Baptist Church and Antioch Baptist Church and brings a wealth of knowledge to Watts Grove Missionary Baptist Church, where she has been the pastor for 16 years. During her time as pastor, Dr. Erwin has established many new ministries, including the New Members Ministry, Married Couples Ministry, Singles' Ministry, Youth Church, Usher/Greeters Ministry, Technology-Media Ministry, Help Ministry, Finance Budget Ministry, Pastoral Assistance Ministry, Dance Ministry, Children's Nursery, Intercessory Prayer, Mother's Ministry, and The Rev. Wanda E. Dae Scholarship.

Dr. Erwin holds several notable achievements, including being the first female pastor at Watts Grove Baptist Church, the first female vice-moderator of the United Missionary Baptist Association, and the first female moderator of the United Missionary Baptist Association. She earned a Bachelor of Theology and Bachelor of Divinity from Teamers School of Religion at Central Community College, a Bachelor of Arts in Religion and Philosophy (Magna Cum Laude) from Shaw University, a Master of Arts in Christian Education from Pfeiffer University, and a Doctor of Ministry from New Life Theological Seminary. Her Doctoral dissertation was, "Why Believe in the Baptism of the Holy Spirit?"

Dr. Erwin has a long list of achievements and awards, including the Scholarship Honors Award, Leadership Training Award, Citation of Recognition Community Service Award, membership in the Alpha Chi National College Honor Scholarship Society, Academic Achievements Awards from 1944-1996, Bronze, Silver, and Gold Academic Medals, Dean's List recognition, as well as being listed in Who's Who of American Women and Who's Who of American Women Leaders. She has also shown dedication and loyal support to the Women's Baptist Home and Foreign Missions of North Carolina Young Adults. Dr. Erwin is a dedicated educator; demonstrated through her commitment to teaching God's Word. She has created classes for Deacons, Deaconesses, Leaders, and Teachers and is committed to outreach and evangelism in the community. She also encourages youth through programs such as Grove Fest, Youth Explosion, Harvest Festival, and Youth Summer Camp.

Dr. Erwin has two children: the late Rev. Wanda Erwin-Dae and Johnny Maurice Erwin, Sr. She also has five grandchildren: Keyetta, Takeisha, Kristina, Taylor, and Johnny Jr., as well as six great-grandchildren.

Dr. Erwin continues to be a dedicated pastor, teacher, and leader; passionate about serving the kingdom of Jesus Christ. She guides under the leadership of the Holy Spirit and is best described as a Trailblazer for Christ. She believes that God will take care of her; and through it all, she trusts in God. The Lord is her Shepherd.

"Be still and know that I am God."
Psalm 46:10

My Journey: Embracing God's Calling

I was called by God during a time when not many female ministers were being ordained in the Baptist churches. Women who were called by God were discriminated against and not respected like the male ministers or preachers. Back then, women struggled to move their roles from missionary leaders, choir leaders, and ushers to the role of ministers. They were not free to use their God-given gifts to fulfill their calling to preach. I had to embrace my calling from God despite others doubting it. I did not have mutual respect or equal opportunity to preach from the pulpit. I was made to feel less than a preacher of the Gospel; only given an opportunity to preach on Mother's Day or Women's Day.

There were times when I felt unseen, unvalidated, and unheard. I received my call from God while serving at my home church, which I had attended from birth. When I announced my calling to my pastor, the first question he asked was who called me. Then he began to call out names of the elder women in the church, implying that one of them had called me. I explained my feelings and my awareness of my calling. I really didn't know what all that I had experienced meant, but I knew the experiences were beyond normal.

Two weeks later, Hurricane Hugo had navigated through our city, and I was delivering my first sermon titled, "Who Touched Me" from the book of Matthew 9:20-22 while standing on the floor. There was no electricity, and very few people attended. Shortly after, the church voted to license me as a Gospel Preacher. Then, a woman and her son wrote an article in the newspaper stating that women were not supposed to preach. I didn't address the article, but my daughter did, and she placed it in the newspaper, "God calls who He wants to call. No one should deny God." Later, my daughter received her call to preach the Gospel at a different church. My family supported me throughout my ministry, attending church whenever and wherever I preached.

On Sundays, before worship, I used to stand outside the Pastor's office and wait to walk in to enter the pulpit for worship. I did this to prevent any rumors from starting. At that time, I was the only associate minister and as a female, I wanted to avoid any potential ridicule, especially on Sundays. Most Sundays, I would only read the Responsive Reading. I had read it so often that I had learned it and could recite it without the hymnal. At my home church, anything I was asked to do was challenged by those who were against women preaching. In fact, it was the women who complained the most; they threatened not to attend functions or activities if I were preaching. I was asked to preach two nights of a four-night revival; the pastor was told by certain members that they wouldn't attend those two nights. Heartbroken, I accepted the decision that I would not preach; it ended up that we didn't host a revival that year. When my pastor was ill, I visited the sick, taught Bible Study, and any other duties he couldn't perform. I preached funerals for the families who requested my services.

The Deacons would call in visiting preachers to preach for specific Sunday worship services. Some of them would let me share in the worship service, while others would question my participation and even my presence in the pastor's office. Again, I chose to wait outside the office. One or two deacons supported me and allowed me to assist with programs and activities. I served in several ministries without compromise: driving the van, helping the kitchen staff, and setting up for ministry anniversaries. The main problem that members of this church had was having me preaching in the pulpit. The title of Associate Minister scared them to a place that was not comfortable for them.

When the time came when it was necessary for me to leave that church, God led me to a church where the pastor was open to women. The limitations were few, but the challenge to prove myself was always present. The pastor was fair in his decisions to invite females to the pulpit to preach and to have opportunities to teach. In my role as a minister, I met some with approval, while others were not sure. I remain dedicated to the Lord's calling and His work without people's approval; I will never stop embracing God's calling.

On one occasion I was asked to preach at a session for a women's organization. I was so excited that women were recognizing women preachers. Two weeks before the session, I was contacted by one of the sisters who shared with me that they were rescinding the invitation to preach; my name was not big enough for this organization. I was disappointed and didn't understand why someone would invite you to preach and later rescind the invitation. I attended the session because I refused to allow them to cut me out of attending. I showed up to support the other female preacher.

Another disappointing experience I encountered was with the association of which my church was a member. They also invited me to preach during a session. Most of the older pastors didn't agree with the selection committee on choosing me as one of the speakers. The session was held at one of the larger churches in Charlotte, North Carolina. I went knowing some were against me. The time came for me to preach, and I remember walking up to the pulpit. I didn't follow protocol. All the pastors had sat on one side of the church. And all but two went out the door. The door closed behind them, and I began the sermon fast and with fury.

I don't remember the exact scripture; I remember talking about David. I said, "Don't be fooled by size." David was small in stature, and everyone did not believe in David, but God did. Size and looks will sometimes fool the best of us. The church with big lights and large crowds will fool the outside, but the inside is what counts. The message wasn't long, but it sure was loud. Before I finished the sermon, all the pastors walked back in. When it was over, my stepfather in the ministry said to me, "Daughter, you fooled them." As I left the church, many approached me with their cards asking me to call them to get a date to preach at their churches. I replied, "I do not call anyone for a preaching engagement; God will supply places for me to preach."

One of the experiences I encountered in seminary was when the professor would ask a question pertaining to pastoring a church. He would ask the male students and say to me, "Sister you do not need to answer the question pertaining to pastor; chances are you will not pastor." I replied, "I want to answer the same question because I'm in the class and have to be graded accordingly."

I had an opportunity to be a candidate for my home church; my pastor had transitioned, and the church became open. The church considered two candidates: me and a male preacher. He had joined the church when he heard the pastor was ill. His family attended the church, but he was of the African Methodist Episcopal Zion denomination. To become a candidate for the church one must be an ordained Baptist preacher; I had to be ordained as well. Both of us were scheduled to take the test on the same day at the same time. The association gave us different times once the process began. I arrived at the church at the time that was given to me and my mentor. We arrived and waited; no one showed up. I went back home and called the moderator and vice-moderator, who were over the ordination committee, to inquire what happened. I explained that I was there at the given time. The moderator replied, "The test is over." I asked when I could take the test, explaining that I had already given my family the date and time of my ordination. The moderator said, "The only time you can take the test is one hour before the ordination service." I agreed but then asked, what would happen if I didn't pass? His response was, "Then, you will not be a part of the ordination service."

The committee was so sure I would fail the written test that they took off for punctuation and anything they could question me on. However, the oral test was perfect. They couldn't fail me, but they tried. Being sure that I wouldn't pass; they didn't even prepare the ordination papers to give me after the service. A year later, I received my ordination papers. However, this only occurred after calling them, leaving numerous messages, and riding to the church to request my ordination certificate.

My last call was not to the moderator, not to my mentor, but to one pastor who believed I deserved to have my ordination paper; I had passed the test. He made it happen and picked up my ordination papers, signed by all the committee. Once the process for pastor began, the deacons of the church met with me to ask me to step down and let the man have the position without a vote. They were going to announce that I had agreed to let him have the church and take over as pastor.

The reason that they suggested this was that they felt that none of the churches in the association would fellowship with them if I became the pastor of the church. However, there were members of the church who supported me. Since I refused to take the offer to step down, all the pastors in the association met with the church and supported the male candidate. The vote was held at the church. I lost the vote, and he won overwhelmingly, but he didn't last as pastor. Due to financial troubles, the church no longer exists. All were hurt by the news. The church was paid off during the previous pastorate. We buried the mortgage going into our new church. Now, the church is non-existent due to a lack of strong administration.

God allows some things to happen to us when we go ahead of Him and not with Him. God moves in a mysterious way. Things don't work like we want them to, but we can always see God working for our good. As a result of everything that happened to me during my journey, I learned to embrace God more. I learned to embrace my journey, *for this journey is not given to the swift or strong, but to the one who endures to the end.* God is not finished with women yet. For the number that did not accept us, there is another number that will. God is calling the church to a new vision- one that does not have a male-only theology.

Women, when God calls you, say "YES". Women are called and will be called. I have been through struggles, pain, and sorrow, but I'm glad I stayed the course. When you recognize God's voice, all other voices don't matter; God overrules them all. I had some pain, but God soothes all the pain. I have shed many tears, but God wipes all of them away. I may still cry at times, but it's a cry of joy with Jesus.

Men pastors who were against me didn't kill me; they certainly tried to hush me up but couldn't keep me down. The hurt was overwhelming; so much to bear. When you are overlooked, it's hard to keep going, and often you will find yourself saying, "What's the use?" One pastor once told me what to say; I was to give quick remarks. He said, "We will let her say hello." He was surprised when I stood and only said "hello" to the congregation. They couldn't believe I did that. It was funny to them, but I was serious. Another pastor said, "When you pray, don't pray too long; it's time to go." I was always led by the spirit. If God said to me to make a remark that was more than "hello", I did. So, if God said to pray as long as I needed to, I did so. God's voice led me to follow His directions. You must embrace God's calling and His voice; other voices can confuse you and make you think God is not in your calling. It takes the power of God to keep you when others are trying to destroy you. It's about power; most want power to destroy, not power to unify.

When I was elected as pastor of Watts Grove and my installation service was announced, invitations were sent to churches in the county association. There were only two pastors that attended. The association didn't want Watts Grove to elect a female pastor. I was okay with that because the pastors in the city where I lived, did attend. In addition, the congregations of both my home churches attended as well.

In 2016, I almost gave up at the death of my daughter. She was my youth pastor and my preaching partner; Rev. Wanda E. Dae was my best friend. She traveled with me to ministers' conferences in Hampton, Virginia, and Dallas, Texas, and the E.K. Bailey Expository Conference in Dallas, Texas, and the How Can They Preach Conference in New Jersey. Since her death, I haven't attended either of these conferences. I always plan to attend, but when the time comes, I can't bring myself to attend. She died while I was at the Hampton Ministerial Conference, but God kept placing my calling before me. I kept embracing my call and continued to think about how far God had brought me, how God kept my mind, how God kept me on course. I couldn't bring my daughter back, but God called my two great-grandsons (twins) to preach the Gospel at the early age of seventeen.

I was overwhelmed with grief. My mother and father died during this time. They all witnessed my calling and my preaching. I made a vow to the Lord; I will embrace my calling, agree with God, and respectfully use my gifts of preaching and teaching for His kingdom and His glory. With purpose, you will be persecuted but we have God to see us through. God be praised for the great things He is doing with us women.

Around Christmas time in 2023, when families were celebrating, exchanging gifts, eating dinner, singing, and visiting family, my family received some terrible news. My great-granddaughter was murdered. We were robbed of her dreams of graduating high school, attending college, and having a family. Again, I kept the faith and accepted the decision of God. Tzion transitioned to heaven. I continued to embrace my calling and preached through pain and sorrow. I still have hope. God is still good. Heaven is in my view. I have a journey to travel through.

Where God has purpose, we must praise. Praise God for whom all blessings flow, God deserves all the praises. He didn't have to call me, but he did. He didn't have to anoint me to preach the Gospel, but he did. He didn't have to save me, but he did. God chose me and other women to preach; not many wise, not many educated, not many chosen. But God chose women, and when God chooses, God uses. God be glorified. Sisters in Christ- Preach!

Tell somebody- *Christ lives and they can live, too!* I heard the voice of Jesus say, *Come unto Me and rest; lay down thou weary one, lay down thy head upon My breast, I came to Jesus as I was rejected and despised, weary and worn and sad. But in Christ, I found a resting place, and now I am truly glad.* But that's not all because I heard Christ say, "*Behold, I freely give, the living water, thirsty one, stoop down and drink and live. I stooped down and drank of that life-giving stream, and my thirst was quenched, my soul revived, and now I live in Jesus Christ! Jesus the Savior of whom so ever will.*" (Para-phrased: Psalms and Hymns to the Living God #327. Author- Horatius Bonar)

It's with joy that I write these pages for others to know that God is still calling women!

Tribute to the Legacy of the Late Reverend Wanda E. Dae

Higher than the sky, deeper than the ocean, more than you even dared to dream. You were wonderfully made with a purpose and a plan for your good. You were fully known by many, completely accepted, and loved by many, more than you could have ever imagined. We will always love you for the time you put in with us and for what you shared with us. You taught us to love by loving us. I never will forget you.
~Dr. Betty J Erwin (Mama)

SALUTING BLACK WOMEN PREACHERS WHO LIVED THE CALL

The biographical sketches are quoted directly from Candice Benbow's article, "Black women preachers who changed-and are changing-history" (Benbow, 2022). They each reflect historical witness of the resilience and current expression of a courage that must be fueled by the Holy Sprit's power and presence.

> *Jarena Lee (1783-1864) - The first woman recognized as a preacher in the African Methodist Episcopal Church. Also, the first African American Woman to publish an autobiography, "The Life and Religious Experience of Jarena Lee, a Coloured Lady, Giving an account of her call to preach the gospel," was first released in 1836.*
>
> *Rebecca Jackson (1795-1871) - Rooting her feminism deeply within her faith, Rebecca Jackson was a writer and religious activist who believed God endowed men and women equally. Her creation of a Shaker community for Black women and her fierce advocacy of egalitarianism made her one of the most controversial religious figures of her time. Her autobiography, "Gifts of Power: The Writings of Rebecca Jackson," is considered one of the most important spiritual autobiographies of all time.*
>
> *Julia Foote (1823-1901) - Julia Foote was the first Black woman to be ordained a deacon with the African Methodist Episcopal Zion Church. Later, she was elevated to the office of elder, becoming the second woman within the denomination to hold that distinction. Foote's autobiography, "A Brand Plucked from the Fire: An Autobiographical Sketch, is noted for its discussion of mental health as Foote chronicles her experience as a Black preaching woman.*

Chapter 3

Rev. Chanetta Lytello-Farmer

Rev. Chanetta Lytello-Farmer

Rev. Chanetta Lytello-Farmer was born on September 20, 1962, in Raleigh, North Carolina, to Ida R. B. Lytello and Warnello Lytello. She was raised in the home with her grandmother Ada Bell Brewer, who was instrumental in her spiritual development.

Rev. Chanetta accepted the Lord as her savior during the first 24-hour marathon at Laodicea United Church of Christ and was baptized under the pastoral leadership of the late Rev. Dr. D.A. Peace. She accepted the call to ministry under the pastoral leadership of the Late Rev. George Hawkins. She was licensed and ordained under the pastoral leadership of Rev. Dr. Joe L. Stevenson.

She was educated in the Wake County Public School System and graduated from N.B. Broughton Sr. High School. She has earned an Associate of Science degree in Early Childhood Development from Wake Technical Community College, a Bachelor of Arts in Liberal Studies with Concentrations in Education and Sociology from Shaw University, a Master of Divinity Degree from Shaw University Divinity School, Master of Education in Educational Leadership from Concordia University. Rev. Chanetta is currently pursuing a Doctor of Ministry Degree in Church Leadership from Hood Theological Seminary. She is a member of both Alpha Chi National Honor Society and Phi Theta Kappa National Honor Society.

Rev. Chanetta currently serves as an associate minister at Macedonia New Life Church in Raleigh, North Carolina. She is also the minister of prayer and the president of the Intercessory Prayer Ministry. She considers intercessory prayer to be an integral part of her ministry. She also worked in Youth Ministry under the then Youth Pastors, Ron and Kim Waldon. She also worked in Youth Ministry while at First Congregational Church. She taught both Teen Sunday School and Teen Bible Study. Rev. Chanetta developed lasting relationships with her students in the church and school system. She has been active in Youth Ministry virtually since accepting the call into ministry. She believes that at her core, Youth Ministry will always be close to her heart.

She is a teacher outside of the church world. She began teaching as a preschool teacher at Learning Together. She became a lead teacher at Wake County Head Start, and from there, taught at Christian Faith Child Development Center and Christian Faith Academy. Currently, she is a substitute teacher at Wake County Public Schools. She has led Trainer-to-Trainer Workshops for UNC-TV. She also accepts outside preaching engagements.

She is the proud mother of three adult sons—Christopher Lytello, who is married to Tranean, and who has blessed her with two grandchildren, Octavia and Ashtyn. Sons, Michael and Jonathan Farmer are the dynamic duo. These three sons are who she calls her "Three Heartbeats."

The scripture that guides her life is Jeremiah 29:11 (TLB)
"For I know the plans I have for you, says the Lord.
They are plans for good and not for evil,
to give you a future and a hope."

Fit for Service:
God Called Me & That's Enough!

For those whom he foreknew he also predestined to be conformed to the image of his Son, in order that he might be the firstborn within a large family. And those whom he predestined he also called, and those whom he called he also justified, and those whom he justified he also glorified. Romans 8:29-33 (NRSVU)

As I look back over my life, I see a story that is far from being a fairy tale. I, like most little girls, dreamed of an idyllic life. I would be married to my Prince Charming, have two kids, a nice house, and a dog. This was the fairy tale. As I awoke to the reality of life, I would find a much different story. The story I would come to understand was one not of my own construction but one that was written and orchestrated by none other than the one who is the author and finisher of my faith. This story has as its author, the creator of the universe. Which is to say that through every crook and valley, He was always there protecting and keeping me in spite of it all. Whenever there was a detour, rocky patch, or anything else that caused discomfort, He was there keeping me.

My start in ministry began with me teaching Sunday School to youth at Laodicea United Church of Christ. As I look back at this period in my life, I am amazed that even at that age, as a teenager, I was sitting at the table with adults. Even then, I did not realize there was a call on my life. When I did begin to recognize the call, I did everything in my power to avoid answering. I bartered with God; at least, that is what I tried to do. I promised that I would teach, I would sing, I would do anything rather than preach. But when God has a call on your life, you can run but you cannot hide. My acceptance did not come easily. But when I had run as far as I could and after much prayer and fasting, my answer would finally be, "Yes, Lord, I will do as You have said."

I did my initial sermon at Laodicea United Church of Christ under the leadership of the late Pastor George Hawkins. He was very supportive and made sure I was ready to take this step into ministry. I also placed a call to the Pastor under whom I had come to Christ, The late Rev. Dr. D. A. Peace. He provided sound advice and instruction.

And so, it begins…

When did I first realize that I would be marginalized? I would say it would begin after I became a member of a mega-church. I had heard so many good things about this church. I can honestly say that this is where I developed my love of the scriptures. I was new to this mega-church. I came to this ministry as a single mother. It was the practice of this church that if you had children who would be in children's church you had to volunteer to work in the children's ministry. I did just that. It was here that again my love of youth ministry would become my passion. I worked in youth ministry until my son aged out. I took a job working in the child development center where I was now getting a paycheck for working with children. I worked there for one year. Then, I became a teacher in the brand-new Christian Academy. I started out as a kindergarten teacher, moved up to being a K-1st grade teacher, on to second grade, Middle School English teacher, and finally a High School English teacher. Also, during this time, I worked as an administrative assistant. I would teach during the day, and at the end of classes, I would go into the administrative offices to work there. For the next 16 years, I worked as both a teacher and as an administrative assistant. Outside the church, I would accept ministry engagements. In terms of ministry here, except for Youth Ministry, I only ministered in the music department. I would sing with the choir and sometimes I would sing special music. This was a solo before the preaching time.

When the place of healing became the source of my pain.

This ministry is where I developed my knowledge of scripture, and it is also the place where I experienced a dark night of my soul. What is a *dark night of the soul?* The phrase, *dark night of the soul* is often used informally to describe an extremely difficult and painful period in one's life.

I have never been a size 8. Maybe when I was a child but while at this church and phase of my life, I definitely was not. That became a problem for one of the Pastors. I was talked about in sermons so much that on one Sunday, another member actually turned around during the message and said, "That's you, isn't it?" I was mortified; I was hurt and had no recourse. I couldn't say anything to the Pastor; that just wasn't done. So, I endured and suffered in silence. Because I was on the payroll and I needed the paycheck, I remained silent.

One day I came to the office and was handed a mandate from the Pastor. It stated that I could not use the elevator anymore, I had to use the stairs. I could not drink soda and I could only eat salads while at work. To make sure I was adhering to the edict, I had people watching me. To ensure that I complied, I decided that I would eat before going to work and not eat again until I was off work. This went on and on for several years. The only things I was allowed to do in ministry were to teach the children, work in the administration office, and occasionally I was allowed to sing. This continued until I left this ministry and joined the church where my then-husband became Minister of Music.

I thought that the pain would be over. Not only because I was married to the Minister of Music, but these people were friends. We were friends before they became pastors. We prayed together, went on fasts together, and our children were friends. Yet, when it came to upfront ministry, I was not able to participate. Again, weight was the reason. This time, the pain was doubled because these were supposed to be my friends. I remained at this church until my marriage ended and I moved back to Raleigh.

Once back in the familiar, I joined the church of one of my friends. I again got into ministry. I joined the Youth Ministry. I became a teacher of the teens. I taught Sunday School, Bible Study, and I was Vacation Bible School Director for two years. I implemented the *Stir Up the Gift Program*. This was to give the youth who were not involved with any ministry a chance to use their gifts. Now, children who had never taken part were signing up to minister. I implemented the *Back-to-School Backpack Drive* for our children. We gave away over 100 book bags to the children of the church, as well as to children within the community. All seemed to be going well until I met with the Pastor to find out what I needed to do in order to preach in his church.

During the discussion, the Pastor told me that I had more outside invitations than the other ministers. He then said that I was doing a great job teaching the children and when I lost weight, he would know that I was ready to preach. I did not then, nor do I now, know what weight had to do with preaching. I remember thinking, "*Does God have separate heavens for skinny people and plus-sized people? Why was it that only plus-sized women were marginalized while plus-sized men were left to minister freely?*" To be quite clear, I still don't know the answer to these questions. I know of several plus-sized male preachers who have no problems preaching. They are pastors and instructors and are accepted based on their gifts and not on their appearance.

I continued there in this new ministry, and all seemed to go well. Teenagers began to come to my class. They were taking the Word seriously. They became tithers. They would come with testimonies of how they had seen God work in their lives. And then I said I was going to Seminary. This is when the bottom fell all the way out. There was a contention because the pastor had not gone to seminary. He had not followed through even though he had agreed to go when he took the position as Pastor. This was a United Church of Christ and one of the mandates in the organization was that to become ordained, one must have a Master of Divinity degree. This all came to a head when the church was debating leaving the UCC. That omission became a talking point with those members who wanted to stay in the UCC.

Once it was decided that the church would leave the UCC, my going to seminary, literally put a target on my back. There suddenly was a need to send monitors into my class during Sunday School and Bible Study. I was called into meetings and had to defend myself against rumors. As God would have it, there was always a witness that vindicated me. I was told that going to seminary would kill my anointing. Why would I want to go to seminary and lose the anointing? My only reply was, *"If I was anointed, attending the seminary would not cause me to lose it!"*

I was stripped of all my duties and told that unless I met with the lead minister, I could not do anything else in the church. I went to the Pastor and requested a meeting to figure out what was going on. He refused to meet with me unless I first met with the lead minister. I had already had one meeting with her and when I was able to produce a witness that would refute all accusations, I was told not to speak of the meeting or God would punish me. Once I stopped teaching the children that I had ministered to, they began to stop coming. I had Deacons coming to me, asking me to take the meeting, and parents coming to me saying that at the next church meeting, they would stand up for me. This, however, was not the case.

Again, I reached out to the Pastor and asked for a meeting. I expressed that I felt like I did not have a covering and that I could not remain uncovered. He had his secretary send me a letter that said, "You are released from your membership." There was no thank you for the work I had done. I wrote and directed Christmas plays, Easter plays, and instituted *Resurrection Boxes* for the children. No acknowledgement was given for anything that I had done. I was devastated! I began searching for another church because I needed a covering. I would not become a Lone Ranger preacher.

A place called home…

WOUNDED AND SEARCHING

This began the search for a new church home. I tried several churches and none of them settled in my spirit. I was looking for somewhere I could rest. I was trying to overcome all the hurt. I was seeking recovery from the broken promises; all the work I had done on the premise that I would be given positions that never materialized. I would still get invitations that I would accept. I would minister while bleeding. I still did not have a church home. I also had to deal with my student colleagues who were Pastors who would say, "I am going to invite you to my church." Later, I found out that they were only trying to get me to assist them with schoolwork. That is one of the reasons I detest group projects to this day.

I was still in contact with many of the young people I used to minister to. It would be one such individual that would be the reason I would finally find my church home. I was trying to get this individual to come back to church. She finally agreed to go with me. She picked the church, and the time was set. We were going to Macedonia New Life. I agreed to go with the understanding we would sit in the back and would leave as soon as the benediction was done. That Sunday would prove to be the turning point for that season of my life. That Sunday morning worship service was explosive! I still remember the sermon that was preached on that day, *"The Invisible Hand of God is Working in Your Life"*. The preacher was dynamic in his presentation. Prolific in his proclamation. It felt like he was only talking to me at that moment. God had backdoored me into showing up at the right place at the right time. When the invitation to unite with this Branch of Zion was given, I united with this new Church. I did not rush to join any ministry. My promise to myself was that this time, I would trust nobody. This time I would not become close to the leader. I would quietly come to church, sit in the back, and leave when the benediction was given. However, when God has a plan, His plan always supersedes your plan.

It would be here that scars would begin to heal. Bleeding places would begin to form scabs of healing. Some healing would come from reconnecting with old friends. Friendships that were forged from childhood. Some healing would come from this Leader who was truly a covering. Some healing would come from finding a place of acceptance. Healing would come in the form of encouragement to pursue the Master of Divinity degree. Here, it was okay to be educated and to be a woman in ministry. It was okay to just be me. Let me be candid. Being home was not a fairy tale happy ending. It was not tiptoeing through a field of roses. It was still something of a proving ground.

There are still older members who, for whatever reason, only see me as Minister Farmer, even though I have fulfilled all the requirements to be called Reverend. I have achieved a Master of Divinity degree, and I have gone through the process of becoming ordained. I have, in fact, completed a second master's degree, and I am working on my Doctor of Ministry degree. I am called by God to preach; I have the education that confirms that call, and yet it is still hard for some to recognize.

What does all this mean to me now? It simply means this… It must be me accepting me. Me believing that I am worthy. Me stepping out of the opinion of others and moving toward relying on the opinion of God. Psalms 139:13-14 (NRSVU) *"For it was you who formed my inward parts; you knit me together in my mother's womb. I praise you, for I am fearfully and wonderfully made. Wonderful are your works; that I know very well.* I am who I am by the Grace of Almighty God. He made me and formed me into His image. I only pulled out a few verses from Psalms 139, but I would encourage you to read the entire Psalm. God knows who you are, and He knows every step you will take. Always remember that in the eyes of God, YOU ARE ENOUGH and YOU ARE FIT FOR SERVICE. God knows who you are and has called you by name. That makes you good enough no matter what your frame looks like.

These are five things I pray you are able to take away from this reading...

1. You are qualified for whatever God has called you to do. *We are confident of all this because of our great trust in God through Christ. It is not that we think we are qualified to do anything on our own. Our qualification comes from God.* 2 Corinthians 3:4-5

2. Always remember God knows who you are. *Before I formed you in the womb I knew you, and before you were born, I consecrated you; I appointed you a prophet to the nations.* Jeremiah 1:5

3. Begin to see yourself as the image of God you were created to be. *So, God created man in his own image, in the image of God created he him; male and female created he them.* Genesis 1:27

4. Love yourself. No one will love you until you love you. It is in loving yourself that you become comfortable in who God made you. Not being arrogant and prideful but celebrating who you are called to be as you seek to fulfill the call of God on your life. There is a song that simply says...*I am who I am today because God used my mistakes.* You are not damaged goods. You are not an accident waiting to happen, you have purpose, and it is up to you to complete your assignment. So, as it says in Proverbs 4:23, "*Above all else, guard your heart, for everything you do flows from it*".

5. Stop being AFRAID. *"I hereby command you: Be strong and courageous; do not be frightened or dismayed, for the Lord your God is with you wherever you go."* Joshua 1:9 You never have to be afraid about not being enough, or not fitting in someone else's mold or idea of what you should look like. The omnipotent omnipresent great God of heaven and earth has fully equipped you for the call.

Always remember you are Fit to Serve and You are Enough!

Chapter 4

Rev. Dr. Katrina Futrell

Rev. Dr. Katrina Futrell

Destined to lead, purposed to empower, and uniquely positioned by God's grace.

Reverend Dr. Katrina Futrell accepted Jesus Christ as her Savior in 1989, at the age of nineteen. In 1998, she had acknowledged her call to the Gospel Ministry and was licensed that next year, in August of 1999. Since that day, she has continued to grow and nurture her God-given gift to preach and teach the Gospel of Jesus Christ.

A hardworking woman of God from meager beginnings, Dr. Futrell has not only built a stellar personal reputation but an outstanding ministerial record as well, one of integrity and faithfulness to the Word of God. It is because of this dedication that she has been able to amass an impressive record of many "firsts" in her local community. At Newsome Grove, Rev. Katrina Futrell became only the second female to be licensed, the first female to be ordained (2008), the first Assistant Pastor (January 2009), and the first female Interim Pastor (February 2018). Just one year later, in February 2019, she was overwhelmingly voted into office as the first female Pastor in the 127-year history of the Newsome Grove Missionary Baptist Church. During her God-led leadership of four years, God brought the Church to a revitalized and thriving place of love, fellowship, and increasing membership.

For every glass ceiling, God allows her to break, she is first and foremost grateful to the Father for the honor and opportunity to do so. Sharing her own knowledge and wisdom, she also supported a host of aspiring Ministers, Evangelists, and fellow Pastors across her hometown community (Northeast). It is truly her belief that God makes room for the gifts of all men and women whom He deems to be not only called but chosen.

Rev. Dr. Futrell has earned professional and ministerial degrees: among them are a Bachelor of Science Degree in Accounting, a Master of Education in Curriculum & Instruction, and both a Master of Art in Teaching/Business Education and a Master's of School Administration (East Carolina University). Ecumenically, she has a Bachelor of Divinity Degree (from Roanoke Theological Seminary) and a Master and Doctor of Ministry Degree (from Grace Bible College and Theological Seminary). She currently studies for her Doctor of Philosophy in Leadership Studies (NC A&T University).

She has served for over 25 years in ministerial and professional leadership simultaneously. She is the founder & President of Amazing Grace Bible College & Theological Seminary, Inc. through a partnership with North Carolina Theological Seminary, Inc.

Rev. Dr. Futrell has served faithfully in multiple roles within Associations and on Councils, Committees, and Boards, as well as pertinent roles with The General Baptist State Convention, Inc. of North Carolina. She has served as Director of Career & Technical Education with both Hertford County and New Hanover County Schools. She looks forward to sharing her experiences at the collegiate level and upcoming ministerial pursuits.

She is a devoted and proud mother of two wonderful children, Kandyce, and T.J., and one fantastic grandson, Monty. She is humbled God chose her to preach and teach the Good News of Jesus Christ and lives life by her favorite passage of Scripture, Isaiah 40:31, *"But they that wait upon the Lord shall renew their strength; they shall mount up with wings as eagles; they shall run, and not be weary; and they shall walk, and not faint."*

To connect with Rev. Dr. Futrell
Facebook: @Katrina Futrell
Email: kfutrell4031@gmail.com

On Eagle's Wings

The Seed of Rejection

In my peripheral vision, I noticed a large cow moving towards me at a slow, deliberate pace, its massive frame swaying from side to side, with each weighty step leaving deep impressions in the earth beneath its hooves. My heart began to beat with great intensity as panic seized my body, rendering me motionless and voiceless. I tried to move, to scream with every fiber of my being, but it was too late; the cow was pressing in hard with its nostrils against my cheek, mooing through the bounds of a muzzle with its hot breath grazing my face.

I strained my brain as to reasons why I was unable to cry aloud for help, why I was rendered voiceless, my mind racing, seeking people who might be able to rescue me from this obnoxious beast… even the cow with a muzzle was able to make sound, yet I was not able to make a sound. Suddenly, my eyes opened, and I realized this was yet another of the same dream, leaving me with a sense of real feelings of intermittent danger, feelings of fear, being alone, voiceless, and powerless, again…

Allow me to pull back the curtains of my childhood and share as a stepchild, that the seed of rejection was implanted in my life for many years. The unmerited verbal harshness, the silencing with physical threats, and the disparity of care caused emotional abuse that triggered the shedding of tears well into my young adult life. I recall vividly a few weeks before the school year started, $300 was given for school clothes with firm instructions that "this should be enough for the three children". My mother bought enough clothes for my three siblings to show that she had followed those orders at least somewhat, as she made sure to "sneak and buy" me at least one pair of pants and a pair of $3 Oxford white sneakers. A pattern of decisions such as this one, coupled with abusive discipline, caused such despair in my life that the feelings of unworthiness to be loved, underserving of being chosen, low self-esteem, and self-doubt became deeply rooted in my soul.

My mother, voiceless and powerless, did her very best to strike a balance between pleasing a spouse and doing right by a child. She fought to find worth in her own life after working odd jobs while being a homemaker. Many years later, she expressed her feelings of being treated as "no more than a child herself". Through years of waiting, increased faith, and confidence, she later found her voice and the courage to become a nurse, wherein she could earn her own money and make decisions that aligned with her heart and own convictions. By this time, I had just completed high school and was strongly encouraged to live with my grandparents temporarily.

As a child, I never understood the dreams that left me paralyzed with fear, alone, voiceless, and powerless --- the place I often reference as beneath the bottom until the call...

The Call – From Beneath the Bottom

From the moment I was called to ministry, there was a sense of divine affirmation that resounded through the halls of my soul. The plot of the enemy had been exposed. The childhood dreams of being voiceless and powerless, the seeds of rejection sown to silence me, were all intended to prevent me from discovering the greater purpose for my life. Witnessing my mother's struggle to find her voice and worth only strengthened my resolve to overcome my childhood struggles and not let them dictate my future. I was not destined to remain in the bottomless place...

The sharing of my call to my pastor was a tearful revelation met with acknowledgment of God going before me and sharing with the pastor that I was called to the Gospel ministry- a clear recognition that a higher power had already ordained my path. Yet, this clarity did not shield me from the complexities that lay ahead. Like the biblical story of Saul and David, our relationship was a dance between support and scrutiny, a reflection of the tensions inherent in spiritual leadership.

In the sanctuary of the church, where one would expect solace and support, I found myself navigating a labyrinth of voices- some supportive, others steeped in tradition and resistance. The men and women wielded their influence, their voices mingling with whispers of doubt that echoed through the pews. It was a struggle to stay true to myself amidst the dissonance of expectations and misconceptions.

Misunderstood and misinterpreted, I found myself at odds with the very fabric of the community I sought to serve. Rumors swirled like a tempest, casting shadows on my intentions and distorting the messages I sought to convey. One incident in particular, a sermon of spiritual warfare entitled, "There is a War Going On!" was interpreted by male leadership as a war for the women to overthrow the Church. Nonetheless, the pastor approved my vision to develop a ministry for the women of the church and community.

This approval came amid rumors that I was convincing, or better yet coercing, all women to believe they were called to preach the Gospel. The Women's Ministry had a profound impact on the women, leading to life-changing experiences. However, its significance often puzzled the men, who frequently sent a deacon to "watch over us" during our meetings that often lasted late into the night. For the men, it was bewildering to think the Spirit of God was moving amongst the women, breaking chains, delivering souls, and setting the hostages free during this "women's ministry". For the record, there are several women preaching and teaching the Gospel to this day, just as God revealed many years ago. Additionally, others have grown in their faith and remain steadfast, working in various roles within the Kingdom of God.

The opportunity to preach the Gospel was far and few in between at my home church. I recall my gift being hindered in ministry at the altar; I was allowed to anoint with oil and move to the next person, but I was not permitted to pray for anyone or share, even if God instructed me to do so. I became what I call an everlasting "Worship Leader" for my home church, as this was the one thing that I was allowed to do the majority of the time.

The pulpit, once a place of empowerment, became a battleground where approval was fleeting and reprimand ever-present. It would be unfair to only speak of the barriers of my male counterparts; the women may have been much harsher, insisting that my attire consist of church hats, dollies, long dresses, and the like. Certainly, I was always dressed in professional attire. Even when I sought counsel in advance with the pastor and received no objections, secret voices lifted with traditions of mankind, and the tables turned as though conversations had never taken place. In the face of adversity, I began to shrink into myself, seeking solace in the confines of my perceived place. But God's voice, unmistakable in its clarity, reminded me that my place was not defined by the constraints of tradition but by the calling placed upon my heart- a calling that spoke of a prophetic destiny to catalyze change and challenge the status quo.

This challenge presented itself in my home, where a call for a wife to evangelize was acceptable, but I would learn years later that the shadow of resentment lurked and built against a wife's call to pastor. The "then" spouse, announced his call to the ministry about one year after my license to preach, only to be rejected by the pastor. This did not make my journey any easier as my call was received and accepted by the pastor as being God-ordained, whereas the pastor unequivocally rejected the call of my then-spouse. This immediately caused tension in the home and led us to step away from the church for four months, a period marked by confusion and conflict. It felt as though I had to choose between my calling and maintaining harmony at home, bearing the burden of bringing both of us through the spiritual door.

I had expressed my desire to attend seminary after my license to preach was administered. My then-spouse insisted that we could not afford it, yet immediately upon his revelation to preach the Gospel, he pursued seminary without regard to the cost. The Spirit of the Lord arose within me, and I found my voice to declare, "Not without me will you attend seminary!" Seminary became both a battleground and a refuge, a space where validation clashed with resistance.

As nine years passed and the battles raged on, I emerged not unscathed but emboldened—a testament to the transformative power of faith and perseverance. The path to ordination was fraught with pressure and politics, a journey marked by moments of doubt and defiance. From the pulpit, innuendos and subtle jabs intensified — particularly the analogy of "if one continues feeding cats, they keep coming back, but if you stop feeding them, they eventually go away." The term "educated fool" was frequently used in sermons, further exacerbating my sense of alienation. The whispers affected my pastor in many ways --- as shared before, this Saul-David, support-scrutiny rapport was grounded in his own insecurities and the whispers behind closed doors.

From the shadows of naysayers and doubters, I transitioned from a licensed minister to an ordained minister (alongside my then-spouse and one other minister). Not long after, the Pastor found his voice and confidence to honor God's mandate to call me as his Assistant Pastor. I rose to assume the mantle of Assistant Pastor, a testament to the indomitable spirit that had guided me through the storm. Yet, through it all, I remained steadfast in my conviction, a beacon of strength and resilience in the face of adversity.

Rest assured; this was not the only place of indignation I endured. There were churches that did not allow women in "their" pulpits. I was often referred to as "*Sister*" versus my male counterparts being called "*Reverend*" or an elevated title of "*Bishop*" or "*Doctor*". The experiences of marginalization endured are too numerous to name and many have been embedded and filed away in the deep crevices of my soul, marked *forgiven*.

Let it be known that there was an unwavering circle of supporters (family, church family, male and female preachers) that embraced me when I was in that bottomless place and still supports me to this day ...

Shattering the Glass Ceiling

The sound of shattering glass reverberates through the corridors of my memory, a poignant reminder of the barriers and limitations that once confined me. As I emerged from one predestined shattering to another, orchestrated only by God, fragments of shattered glass embedded themselves deeply in my soul and spirit. These fragments serve as a constant reminder of the battles fought and the scars earned.

I began attending my home church, Newsome Grove, at the age of 13 years old. I will never forget the kind soul that loaded all the neighbor children in her car and drove us to the "church down the road". Never in my deepest thoughts could I have imagined the plans God had for my life. I became only the second female to be licensed at Newsome Grove. God ensured that I witnessed the first female to be licensed under said leadership, watching the ceiling shattered before my very eyes. As a matter of fact, it was at this occasion that He showed me a vision that I would someday do the same. Of course, I had no clue and discarded the vision, thinking I would never have that many words to say before any audience. One Uncle reminds me, to this date, that he too, prophesied I would preach the Gospel. In total, God allowed four ceilings to shatter at my home church; I was the first female to be ordained (2008), the first female Assistant Pastor (January 2009), and the first female Interim Pastor (February 2018). Just one year later, in February 2019, I was overwhelmingly voted into office as the first female Pastor in the 127-year history of the Newsome Grove Missionary Baptist Church.

As I transitioned to the position of pastor in my home church, I confronted entrenched prejudices and preconceptions that sought to confine me to the margins. The challenge was not just breaking through the glass ceiling but also dealing with the intersectional barriers of race, gender, and religious expectations. Men (and some women) in the church often questioned my role, and societal norms seemed to conspire against my calling. Yet, with each step forward, I refused to be defined by the shards of glass that lingered within, too fine to be removed. I drew strength from the wellspring of my faith, the resilience of my spirit, and a God like no other on my side!

On Eagle's Wings

I firmly believe the epitome of my life is represented in Isaiah 40:31; *"They that wait on the Lord shall renew their strength; they shall mount with wings like eagles."* This type of waiting is not passive but waiting that encompasses confident expectation and active hope in God. I have learned how to wait on God in hope and prayer, allowing Him to exchange my limited strength for His divine strength. And not just wait but wait well while God gracefully mounted me with eagle's wings to soar overburdens and situations that were intended to keep me in a broken place. He allowed people to see the God in me. And this is how I was able to remain true to whom God called and predestined me to become.

It was this same spirit of humility and strength that caused the people of Newsome Grove Missionary Baptist Church to become united and vote the will of God for the ceiling to be shattered. I did not do it alone; it was men and women who stood by my side --- they were part of the process in which God showed forth He is not bound by the words of envious individuals. I pause to give my Church family the homage due.

God selects the oddest of times to mount us with eagle's wings. At the precise moment, I said yes to God's plan in ministry, I also released a 28-year marriage marked by consistent betrayal, with the final act of betrayal publicly displayed in the very church I was called to pastor. In doing so, I embraced the freedom to pursue my pastoral calling. God showed me without a doubt that He had plans for my life; they were plans of hope and a future. It is noteworthy to mention the support my pastor showed during the two-year journey that led to my freedom; I am forever grateful for his support.

I encourage anyone reading this chapter to stay true to who you are in God and trust His process; the testimony of people about you will change over time. And if it does not, let it be well with your soul! God has the final say! Here are a few examples that I share all the time that defied the jealous naysayer who declared, "The deacons will never let you become pastor of that Church"! There was one deacon, initially skeptical of a woman preaching, who became a steadfast supporter, acknowledging the value of my ministry despite societal norms until his passing. A few deacons encouraged me that you just never know what God may do someday, and why not a woman (referring to my becoming pastor). These deacons were strong advocates and supporters of my pastoral ministry. Another deacon expressed doubts about my ability to lead as a divorcee and a woman. Despite his reservations, he stood by me until his death --- his words will forever be etched in my soul- "You have been a mighty good pastor to me." It is noteworthy to mention that the mothers of the Church loved and protected me like their own. There are too many examples to name and too personal to quote but let me share what I know- there were men and women who stood by my side. Whether they stood in the beginning, the middle, or at the end, I am grateful they were able to discern this work is greater than me, and my desire was always to personify Him.

Newsome Grove had endured at least three Church splits and the loss of reputation, known as a Church of love and community amongst the people. It was through my God-led leadership and the people therein that God brought the Church to a revitalized place of love, fellowship, membership, and their call to serve the community regardless of the pain endured. I am humbled by the opportunity to have been a part of the journeys of others, a privilege granted by God's grace.

I was the rejected, the least likely, the written off, the canceled out, the broken, the humiliated, the confused, and abused, but God renewed my strength and mounted me up with eagle's wings! Through my continued journey, I hope to motivate, empower, and educate many others to know their true purpose in life and know that they too, can rise on eagle's wings. This chapter cannot tell the whole story, but I pray regardless of your calling—whether serving as a pastor, preacher, teacher, singer, or usher in the house of God, or pursuing a career as an educator, entrepreneur, manager, librarian, or in any other field it has provided enough to show that if you wait on God in hope, prayer, and faith, you can expect to soar on eagle's wings any day now!

To God Be the Glory for my inner circle: My forever sister, Sonya, by the only blood that matters; my children who are my two heartbeats, Kandyce and TJ; my adorable grandson, Monty, and a very special friend, Karl; my siblings who always loved me as their big sister; Angela (deceased), Lakisha, Lakendria, and James Jr. Last but not least, in loving memory of my mother, Geraldine who wholeheartedly supported me in ministry.

Chapter 5

Rev. Dr. Towanda Garner

Rev. Dr. Towanda Garner

Rev. Dr. Towanda C. Garner is grateful to be a servant of the Most-High God under the pastoral leadership of Rev. Dr. Joe L. Stevenson at Macedonia New Life Church of Raleigh, North Carolina. Rev. Dr. Garner serves as the Youth Pastor for the MAC Youth Ministry at the church. Rev. Dr. Garner's favorite scripture is, "*I can do all things through Christ who strengthens me*" (Philippians 4:13, NKJV). A North Carolina native, Rev. Dr. Garner completed undergraduate studies at East Carolina University, Greenville, North Carolina with a B.A. in Psychology; completed graduate studies at North Carolina Central University, Durham, North Carolina with a M.A. degree in Psychology (Clinical); completed graduate studies at Duke University/Duke Divinity School with a M.A. in Divinity with certificates in Baptist Studies and Black Church Studies; and completed doctoral studies through Andersonville Seminary Theological Institute with a Doctor of Ministry in Christian Counseling (Summa Cum Laude). Rev. Dr. Garner is especially thankful to be an Ordained Minister. She is also a Licensed Clinical Addictions Specialist (LCAS) credentialed by the North Carolina Addictions Specialist Professional Practice Board. Rev. Dr. Garner is employed with The Family Violence Prevention Center as the Therapeutic Services Program Administrator.

Rev. Dr. Garner is a member of the National Alliance on Mental Illness of Johnston County, North Carolina and holds a lifetime membership to Psi Chi Honor Society in Psychology. She is the founder of a 501 (c) (3) nonprofit organization entitled, *United Therapeutic Youth & Family Services, Inc.,* with a primary goal to assist adults, youth and families dealing with issues related to substance use and/or addictions.

Rev. Dr. Garner is the proud parent of Breanna Victoria Garner, a graduating high school senior in the Class of 2024. She will be attending Duke University, Fall 2024.

My Help Comes from the Lord: The Strength Within

HALLELUJAH... I'M FREE FROM IMPRISONMENT! For many years, I suffered from imprisonment that went far beyond a typical 8 x 6 feet windowless, dismal prison cell. I was silently bullied incessantly by devastating, demeaning thoughts that held me captive for decades. The insidious fear of failure also kept me confined in an ominous space - the IMPRISONMENT OF THE MIND...A DARK PLACE THAT I PRAY NEVER TO RETURN. My life's journey into the development of a woman preacher/teacher of the Word of God has encountered some tumultuous days, been filled with some joyful moments, countless tears, and indisputably, some sleepless nights. I prayerfully persevered through the hardships encountered in LIFE with the unwavering help of God on my side...THE STRENGTH WITHIN. Without a shadow of a doubt, I can declare, "When I am weak, God gives me strength."

The immutable word of God states in Ephesians 1:4-5, NIV,
> For he chose us in HIM before the creation of the world to be holy and blameless in His sight. In love, he predestined us for adoption to sonship through Jesus Christ in accordance with his pleasure and will- to the praise of his glorious grace, which He has freely given us in the One he loves.

I could not believe that God had CHOSEN ME to preach and teach the holy word of God. The question reverberated in my mind, "GOD, WHY ME?... I'm full of imperfections and fallibilities. Therefore, to teach the infallible word of God was beyond my comprehension... I'm a broken vessel in need of restoration... WHY ME, GOD? How can my wounds from the past that left scars of shame and guilt promote HOPE to other wounded souls?

As I reflect on my Christian journey of salvation, I think back to the bewildered 17-year-old, twelfth-grade high school student who surrendered her life to Jesus Christ one Sunday morning at church, following my biological father's confession of sin and acceptance of Jesus Christ as his Lord and Savior. Despite achieving academic success in high school and being obedient to my parents, it seemed that I could never achieve my father's validation…his unconditional love. I, therefore, followed in his footsteps to the altar on that Sunday morning hoping to make him proud of me. After several months, my father and I both failed at living the sanctified Christian life as defined by the Church. I grew up in a Pentecostal holiness church; therefore, almost everything was classified as "sin". This was especially true when I started wearing "pants" again. During the summer, I entered my freshman year of college. I was thrilled and anxious to experience the freedom and wonderful joy of being released from the bondage of living with strict parents. I was excited to become acclimated to the college environment. Out of a desire to enjoy my newfound freedom, I failed to actively practice my religious teachings. Instead, I studied hard and became immersed in college life. I'm grateful for God's everlasting love and perpetual protection over my life.

Many of the mistakes I made in life and the misfortunes that I suffered were birthed out of unfortunate childhood beliefs and insecurities. I was told, I'm not worthy…I'm not good enough… I'm not smart enough, I'm not pretty enough. As a result, I couldn't accept that I deserved what was predestined by God, the Almighty, who is omniscient, omnipresent, and omnipotent…God, the creator of the universe and everything within it. God had to teach me through my trials and tribulations in life that:

- Even in my infirmities
- Even with my self-doubts
- Even in my brokenness…

GOD CHOSE ME, and GOD CHOSE YOU TOO! God chose me even before conception in my mother's womb...even before my miraculous birth into the world - I existed in the WILL of GOD. As the Bible states, *"Yes, I have loved you with an everlasting love; therefore, with lovingkindness, I have drawn you."* (Jeremiah 31:3 NLV) We must remember that we are chosen by God and hand-picked to do the work of God. IN OTHER WORDS, BEING CHOSEN IS NOT BY HAPPENSTANCE. IT'S AN INTENTIONAL ACT OF GOD. THEREFORE, IT'S AN HONOR TO BE CHOSEN. Satan is terrified of me and you aligning with the WILL OF GOD because Satan is aware that GREATNESS LIVES WITHIN THE CHILDREN OF GOD. The Bible says, *"For I know the plans I have for you, declares the Lord, plans to prosper you and not to harm you, plans to give you hope and a future."* (Jeremiah 29:11 NIV)

To walk boldly into my calling as a woman preacher, it was necessary to cast the self-deprecating thoughts that plagued me and attacked my mind into the pits of HELL. The thoughts didn't derive from our merciful, loving God but were the voices of the enemy derived from people of the world...the most hurtful comments were from people within my inner circle. To preach and teach the powerful Word of God, under the anointing of the Holy Spirit, I needed to become resolutely secure in my identity:

- As a Black woman
- As a child of God
- As a Christian

It was imperative for me to boldly fight this battle, within my mind, with the powerful words of GOD, written in the scriptures. The words of the Bible became the mighty weapons of warfare I used to dismantle the enemy. Transformation of the mind was pivotal; it required cognitive restructuring of my thoughts because my psyche had been bruised since childhood. I needed to seek restoration from brokenness and wholeness through Jesus Christ in order to fulfill the call of God into the ministry. I was a willing vessel, obedient to do the will of God after so many years of trying to escape the call. I read the word of God; I studied the Bible.

In 2017, I was accepted into Duke Divinity School, Durham, North Carolina, for the word of God says, "S*tudy to show thyself approved to God, a workman that needeth not to be ashamed, rightly dividing the word of truth.* (2 Timothy 2:15, Webster's Bible Translation) I was finally walking in obedience! Although the demeaning thoughts attempted to creep back into my mind, I was determined to do the will of God…THE STRENGTH WITHIN. With the power of the Holy Spirit and the courage deposited in me by my loving Heavenly Father, I valiantly slayed the enemy and was victorious in disputing negative self-talk such as:

- You're not good enough to be a preacher…
- Women are not called to preach… Don't you read the Bible…
- True preachers called by God don't go to Divinity School to learn how to preach…

The words of the enemy were VICIOUS AND DANGEROUSLY AGGRESSIVE, but the Bible says, *"For the word of God is living and active, sharper than any two-edged sword, piercing to the division of soul and of spirit, of joints and of marrow, and discerning the thoughts and intentions of the heart."* (Hebrews 4:12) Women of God, we can't allow the voices of Satan to **bully us out of the pulpit**!!! We must stand firm on our calling by God, go forth and, *"Preach the word; be prepared in season and out of season; correct, rebuke, and encourage - with great patience and careful instruction. For the time will come when people will not put up with sound doctrine."* (2 Timothy 4:2-5 NIV)

My marriage of 15 years was falling apart. In 2014, I was diagnosed with chronic heart disease, therefore, my physical health was compromised. To attend Divinity School (as led by the Spirit Within) full-time, I needed to resign from my job of 12 years. My stable, secure source of income no longer existed, but I faithfully TRUSTED GOD. The profound saying that intensely resonated with me and provided inspiration was, "If

God brings you to it, HE will bring you through it." Therefore, I continued to pray and TRUST IN GOD. I didn't know how Almighty God would bring me through these trials and tribulations, but I was confident I would emerge VICTORIOUS… **THE STRENGTH WITHIN!** Although my faith was under attack, I knew God was leading me through the storms of life.

After weeks of occasionally experiencing moderate difficulties breathing, one day, I struggled to breathe so badly that I went to the emergency room and had to be immediately hospitalized due to Congestive Heart Failure, Cardiomyopathy, and High Blood Pressure. "GOD, What Happened?" I asked in disbelief. I could hear the boisterous laughter of Satan in my head, his devilish voice taunting me, "What are you going to do now, you can barely breathe… it's impossible for you to preach the WORD of GOD?" This was August 2018, the commencement of the fall semester at Duke Divinity School, my second year. What am I going to do now? My answer… **TRUST in GOD** even more so! As the cardiologist revealed the devastating news that my heart had suffered severe damage and the prognosis wasn't favorable, I silently whispered, "God, you brought me too far to leave me now…I have a precious nine-year-old daughter who needs her mother to live and not die!"

I desperately needed to embrace **THE STRENGTH WITHIN**. The cardiologists shared that my life expectancy was approximately five years with the existing medical conditions of my heart unless I acquired a heart transplant. "My GOD, My GOD, speak to ME…I need to hear your voice for guidance before taking action." I waited to hear from God as I was scheduled for extensive laboratory blood work in preparation for a heart transplant. I waited to hear from God…I embraced **THE STRENGTH WITHIN - THE HOLY SPIRIT.**

God didn't instruct me to undergo a heart transplant BUT to change my lifestyle…to eat healthier, to exercise more, and to entertain less stress. The cardiologists respected my decision to WAIT (as God had instructed me to do). The team of cardiologists ordered a medical leave from Divinity School in Fall 2018. They prescribed one of the best heart medications available for treating heart failure and ordered three months of cardiac rehabilitation, once again (first cardiac rehab was in 2016). I had been through heart issues before. In 2015, the surgical implantation of an implantable cardioverter-defibrillator (ICD) was required due to dangerous, life-threatening abnormal heart rhythms (ventricular tachycardia or ventricular fibrillation) that can cause sudden cardiac arrest if the condition is not treated immediately.

We never know how God is going to bring forth healing and/or physical restoration to one's body. As I faithfully attended cardiac rehab sessions, vigilantly monitored my food choices and portion sizes (eat one small slice of cake or no dessert/cake; definitely not three slices at one setting), limited my salt and sodium intake, adhered to my medication regimen for the restoration of my health…my heart began to strengthen! Although GOD makes the ultimate decision regarding our life's existence, the daily choices we make may be a profound determinant in the equation, as well. Each day, I had to seek **THE STRENGTH WITHIN - THE HOLY SPIRIT** (as a teacher, guide, advocate, comforter, and the Spirit of Life) as I struggled along this path to better health.

One night, I distinctly heard the calming voice of the Holy Spirit whisper to me, "**YOU SHALL LIVE AND NOT DIE.**" Almost six years later, I gratefully live with the *heart* God created within me from conception! Sadly, however, in 2019, my 49-year-old younger sister died because of Congestive Heart Failure and Diabetes.

I would like for the people of God to be fully aware that the enemy has a formidable arsenal of weapons to deploy and cunningly attack the children of God; therefore, we must always be watchful and prayerful. Remember, as King David eloquently quoted in Psalms 27:1-3, NIV, *"The Lord is my light and my salvation—whom shall I fear. The Lord is the stronghold of my life—whom shall I be afraid?"* Even when friends, family, your children, co-workers, or your health come against you, don't be afraid, seek **THE STRENGTH WITHIN…THE HOLY SPIRIT.**

I shared my health challenges earlier to say that WE are sometimes our own worst Enemy. Therefore, sometimes, we are held accountable for our reckless behaviors. I consistently abused my body for years by blissfully consuming an unhealthy diet, failing to exercise, and experiencing insufficient rest and sleep. Yet, I forced my body to function unmercifully until the day of reckoning was upon me. To wholeheartedly fulfill the call of God on our lives in ministry, we must respect and honor our temples and love the powerful *Woman* God created us to be. We must value God's call to the ministry as Pastors, Preachers, and Teachers to share and spread the gospel of Jesus Christ. Pray for the naysayers and stand against oppression within the church by refusing to suppress your spiritual gifts and the powerful anointing God has blessed you with. **Don't be bullied by the voices in your head nor the bullies in the pews and the pulpits** who want you to think you're not meant to teach and preach the WORD of GOD because of your gender – being a woman.

As a preacher of color, it's imperative that we remain aware of the deleterious, historical impact of the miseducation and distortion of the Bible by the oppressors on the promotion of colonialism, the perpetuation of slavery, and the subjugation and marginalization of people of color. We, as a people of God, must not do what the oppressors did during slavery: demean, dishonor, and disrespect innocent people. It's time to unify as the body of Christ so that we may glorify the name of Jesus. There's far too much dissension, chaos, and violence in the world for the Church to be embroiled in ruthless conflict regarding the call of women as clergy and holding leadership roles in the Church of Jesus Christ. God is omniscient, omnipotent, omnipotent and reigns supreme; therefore, God has the authority to put into position whomever he appoints and anoints – male or female. People are spiritually dying in the world; the church is being mocked while humanity is discussing and arguing about the validity of women's call into the ministry as pastors, preachers, and leaders by our Sovereign God. Let's be about our Father's business before the people in the world completely self-destruct.

The work of the Lord consists of addressing a plethora of vital issues in a society plagued with hatred, racism, sexism, ageism, food insecurity, homelessness, domestic violence, substance addictions, human trafficking, sexual abuse of women and children within the church, gun violence, school and college shootings (the United States overwhelmingly leads globally), police brutality, and ecocide (environmental crimes). We're dying a slow, gradual death due to the use of commercial-grade highly hazardous pesticides. As a result, the natural environment (wildlife, insects, the soil, plants, the air, etc.) is suffering horrifically. These and many other issues need to be appropriately addressed and eradicated within society before the earth suffers complete destruction and everything within it. There's plenty of work for humanity to accomplish on earth in promoting a healthy and equitable society as we uplift each other throughout the world and within the Church of Jesus Christ as opposed to attempting to discredit one another.

Although women experienced significant roles in ministry during the early Church, their contributions were not readily acknowledged due to entrenched patriarchal and societal beliefs during biblical times. God, however, utilized women in leadership roles within the Church and within society which was contrary to cultural norms at the time. Explicit examples in the Old Testament are:

- Deborah administered justice, served as a prophetess and a courageous military leader who helped to victoriously lead the Israelites in the fight against the Canaanites.

- Queen Esther was bravely willing to sacrifice her life to save her people, the Jews, by having King Ahasuerus (Xerxes I) to withdraw an edict for the killing of the Jews.

Profound examples in the New Testament are:

- Mary Magdalene preached on the resurrected Jesus Christ at a time when women were prohibited from witnessing.

- Anna was a female prophet in the New Testament.

Jesus rejected the cultural customs as illustrated by his utilization of women in ministerial roles and his respectful and compassionate treatment of women in the Bible which appeared to be contrary to Apostle Paul's statements regarding women. It's important to remember that Apostle Paul was an Israelite of the tribe of Benjamin, was raised as a Pharisee, and was a Roman citizen. As a devout Pharisee, his early indoctrination to the Pharisaical Code and the role of women within society were deeply ingrained, one could say. Apostle Paul's perspectives on women's roles in the church are distinctly a reflection of his teachings and training as a Pharisee, perhaps. Such an education would have opposed women in leadership roles and not viewed women as equal to men according to patriarchal cultural customs. The writer of 1 Timothy 2:12, believed by many to be Apostle Paul, states, "*I do not permit a woman to teach or to have authority over a man; she must be silent,*" reflecting the cultural custom he endorsed. It's interesting how Apostle Paul's view of women's roles within the first-century church continues to be controversial in the 21st-century church.

As a woman preacher of the gospel of Jesus Christ, we must do what our Sovereign God has called us to do, for such a time as this. As the Apostle Paul said, "*...Forgetting what is behind and straining toward what is ahead, I press on toward the goal to win the prize for which God has called me heavenward in Christ Jesus*" (Philippians 3:13). We can't afford to become distracted by the voices of the enemy but continue to uplift and glorify the name of Jesus.

As we go forth, I leave with you five strategies to employ:

- Trust in God and know that you have THE STRENGTH WITHIN to support you.
- Network with female and male clergy who support and encourage you.
- Never stop learning and being teachable.
- Learn to say "NO" without guilt.
- Take time to REST, LAUGH, and HONOR THE MIGHTY WOMAN OF GOD YOU ARE.

Lastly, I came across a beautiful prayer entitled, "The Knots Prayer," which may provide HOPE in times of doubt.

The Knots Prayer

Dear God,

Please untie the knots that are in my mind, my heart, and my life.

Remove *the have nots, the can nots and the do nots that I have in my mind.*

Erase *the will nots, may nots, might nots that find a home in my heart.*

Release *me from the could nots, would nots, and should nots that obstruct my life.*

And most of all, Dear God, I ask that you remove from my mind, my heart, and my life all of the "am nots" that I have allowed to hold me back, especially the thought that I am not good enough.

Amen

(Author Iyanla Vanzant)

Chapter 6

Rev. Nichole L. Harris Glover

Rev. Nichole L. Harris Glover

Teach me thy way, O LORD; I will walk in thy truth: unite my heart to fear thy name. I will praise thee, O Lord my God, with all my heart: and I will glorify thy name for evermore." Psalm 86:11-12 (KJV)

Rev. Nichole L. Harris Glover is a mother, minister, missionary, intercessor, visionary, teacher, actress, singer, poet, author, inspirational speaker, entrepreneur, and skilled information technology engineer. A prophet in her own right, she was born the second of three children to the late Kenneth Arnold Harris, Sr. and Mother Carolyn Virginia Levister Harris in Washington, DC, and raised between Prince George's County, Maryland, and Wake County, North Carolina, then relocating to Essex County, New Jersey and Cobb County, Georgia.

Nichole gave her life to the Lord when she was a freshman in high school, as a Senior in college, and again as an adult. As a youth, she participated in multiple youth choirs and church plays. While in college she became active in the community working with the local NAACP, Big Brothers and Big Sisters, and other campus organizations, while helping young people reclaim their self-confidence and hope.

In 2006, Nichole began serving as a Sunday School Teacher for YouTube for ages three to six years, then added service as a youth minister and other ministries to help grow the then-small church. The additional ministries included serving as the Director of the Courtesy Ministry, Co-Head of Security, singing in the choir, mime, praise dancing, acting, serving as camera person for the Audio-Visual Ministry, and server for the Kitchen\Hospitality ministry.

In 2008, she founded *OPTIONS² Inc.*, a 501 (c) 3 non-profit organization with a mission to educate, empower, equip, and encourage the restoration of hope as we navigate through life's transitions so all (youth, families, and former military) will become victorious over their past and present. Through *OPTIONS²*, she provides training, spiritual guidance, and connects the participants with the necessary resources to receive the necessary equipping to move past their circumstances and toward success. The work of *OPTIONS²* has grown across all geographical boundaries, physically and virtually.

Nichole attended North Carolina Central University (NCCU) and earned her Bachelor of Business Administration with a concentration in Computer Information Systems. While at NCCU she served with many campus organizations.

Nichole was ordained on August 26, 2012, as a Minister of the Gospel to Evangelize, Preach, Teach, and Serve God's Kingdom. In pursuit of her ministerial equipping, Nichole continued her journey through academia by earning her M.B.A in Marketing and Project Management from American Intercontinental University (Chicago, IL) and attended Shaw University Divinity School (SUDS), earning her M.A. in Christian Education and her M.Div. While attending Shaw University Divinity School, she has served as the President of the Parent Teacher Student Association of her son's high school; and the Secretary, Vice- President, and President for the Student Government Association at Shaw University Divinity School for three consecutive years, assisted with the organization of the annual women's conference, and established the first Shaw University Divinity School Intercessory Prayer Team. In the midst of COVID, Nichole was requested to serve on the Executive Board of the Wake Missionary Baptist Association, in North Carolina, which she graciously accepted.

Rev. Glover received additional training and certificates in Anti-Crime and Incarceration Ministry, and one in Theology, and one in Hermeneutics from Eastern Carolina Christian College and Seminary. Rev. Glover had multiple articles published relating to organ donation (DonateLifeNC.org), and authored devotionals for the Women's Baptist Home & Foreign Missionary Convention's publication, *Missionary Helper Devotionals*.

Rev. Glover currently serves as the CEO, Visionary, and Facilitator of *OPTIONS^2;* co-host to a daily weekday devotional call at her company (where she works as a Software Engineer); leader of a daily text ministry, reaching people across the country and continents; Adjunct Professor for Christian Education and Creative Worship courses at Easter Carolina Christian College and Seminary; an Associate Minister, Bible Study Teacher, Vacation Bible School Teacher, and an Intercessor at Saint Matthew Missionary Baptist Church; a member of Delta Sigma Theta Sorority, Inc.; and a licensed financial professional. Rev. Glover also was a former massage therapist and a licensed Onyxologist (nail technician).

Rev. Glover often proclaims, next to the gift of life and salvation, one of the greatest gifts God has given to her is to be the mother of her son, who is also a prayer warrior seeking God for continued guidance in his service and ministry.

Psalm 71:7-8 (NLT), "My life is an example to many, because you have been my strength and protection. That is why I can never stop praising you; I declare your glory all day long."

The "S" on My Chest

H ave you ever felt …

felt unloved?	Superfluous
wondered what life would be like without you?	Suicide
struggled with temptation?	Sin
had a desire to serve?	Servant
been in the military?	Soldier
survived Domestic Violence, Diseases, Diagnosis, Molestation?	Survivor
overcome addiction?	Sober
been discounted because of how and /or Single mother raised who you were raised by?	Single Mother
looked out for others more than yourself?	Selfless
had to bear the burdens of others?	Sucked it up
cried alone, so no one would know?	Strong
been an unmarried mom?	Separated\Single Mother
ashamed of what you did?	Stolen/Sold Drugs/Stripped
been struggling, or are struggling with debt?	Student Loans
been overweight?	Super fluffy
wondered who you are supposed to be?	Someone Loved by\Servant of God
felt alone?	Shunned
felt discounted for…?	Sidelined
falsely accused of…?	Smeared
been trapped by "career casting" or a volatile relationship?	Stuck
been raped or brutalized?	Special Victim
been hurt so bad, you blame yourself or God?	Scarred
held in your anger and pain?	Smiled instead of Screaming
been loved and kept unconditionally?	Sufficient Grace
had someone give up their life for you?	Sacrifice
thought about dying to yourself, and living for God?	Surrendering
received a gift that no one can buy?	Salvation
felt a "never forsaking" protection, provision, and love?	SAFE IN HIS ARMS

If you answered "YES" to any of the above questions, you have an ⓢ on your chest. We go through so much as human beings. However, struggles in life are often amplified for certain members of various groups and communities, such as: black, brown, or yellow; females, young soldiers, single mothers and ministers (especially a Preacher). These community impacts are often amplified when ingesting one or all of them into the church. However, our final "S-stination" does not have to be as challenging or trying.

This chapter will illuminate the various transitions and experiences in my life and the different "S's" I wore and hid on my chest. The hope for this chapter is that you (the reader) will be encouraged, enlightened, and equipped to keep on, hold on, and trust in the process called life. Through my reflections, reflect on your own past personal experiences, remembering and recalling the experiences as you seek the lessons in them. Then release anything that has hurt, harmed, scarred, scared, or hindered you from being your BEST (Blessed by the Experiences Survived and Triumphed) self. Allow yourself to be loved, kept, and covered, safe in the arms of our GOD, through His only begotten Son. Finally, know that you have the power to move past your past, and toward your purpose and the promises of God, even if it means you must PRESS *(illuminated at the end of the chapter).*

My journey began at the Columbia Hospital for Women in Northwest Washington, D.C. Though I was born loved by God, my parents, older brother, and extended family, I was still born into sin.

SINNER

As David reminds us in the Bible, in Psalm 51:5, "Surely I was sinful at birth, sinful from the time my mother conceived me." This serves as a reminder we are all born into sin, sinners at birth, not by any choice or action of our own, yet sinners just the same. I always find it interesting how God kept His word to cause the descendants of Adam and Eve to bear their sins. However, God also provides us an OPTION, an alternative to being dead in sin, which is to have "life abundantly" despite sin.

SAFE

This is where HIS grace is magnified! God knows, and knew, the plans He has for us (Jeremiah 29:11). His ultimate goal and desire were that we should not perish or live in lack, we should not be bound or burdened by sin. So, He provided a way for our sins to be forgiven, once and for all. God provided this alternative to living a life of sin, to living a life safe in HIS arms... it is our choice.

SOLDIER

It is also our choice as to whether we will be still long enough to hear the *full* instructions of the LORD or be anxious and jump up to take matters into our own hands. I remember when God was calling me to become *a soldier*. I was in high school and seeking to learn more about who God was to me, what His Word meant to me, and how I could help my family. Up until this point, since the time of my birth, I witnessed and was exposed to:

☐ *So many sheets to the wind* - My Daddy's alcoholism –
My Daddy was a God-Fearing man, handsome, tall, curly-haired, slender, with a deep voice, and big hands. My Daddy had a big heart and love for his wife, children, and family. He was gifted with humor; having the ability to make *anyone* laugh. He was a lover of music; however, he was also the lover of a vice that eventually caused his death. As I grew older, I began to ask myself, what caused him to start drinking in the first place? My Daddy! I love and miss him, so very much! Each time that I think of him, I wonder what I could have done to help save him or to get him to stop drinking. He was the sweetest and funniest man I knew. My protector! He would do anything, go anywhere, and sacrifice anything for his family. However, when he drank… I grew to call him the "Sleeping Giant". All was well unless you awoke him out of his sleep after he had his "after-work taste".

☐ *Screaming and Yelling* - He and my mother arguing –
I remember her, in her nurturing, well-meaning way, would attempt to wake Daddy after he had his "after-work taste" and fell asleep in the chair to get him to go upstairs. Whenever she tried to wake him, it did not seem to ever go well. I recall between the ages of two and four, having the phone numbers of my grandparents, and all my mother's manually written contacts from her phonebook, memorized. *(Please remember, this was long before cell phones, in the early 1970's.)* I would call my Granny (maternal Grandmother) or Grandma (paternal Grandmother) and say, "Granny (or Grandma), will you come help my mommy? Please note, for the record, I never saw, with my own eyes, my Daddy hit my mother, but something in me knew she needed help. I would often wonder why she wouldn't just let him sleep.

☐ _Shook_ - My parents divorced - When I was between my sixth and seventh year of life, my parents were going through the process of getting divorced. I was "shook"! I thought, when the divorce was finalized, it would mean I would no longer have a Daddy. I thank GOD for my Mommy, Daddy, and big cousins, who helped me to understand that was not the case. It only meant that my parents would no longer live in the same house, and I would be able to visit my Daddy in his new house.

☐ _Surrogacy_ - A form of Motherhood before eight years of age. - Our Mommy was working two and three jobs to make ends meet and make sure we did not suffer from a lack due to the divorce. Daddy would still pick us up and take care of us, yet I found myself as a seven-year-old big sister, serving as a surrogate mother, protector, keeper, coverer, cook, and hairdresser of my then five-year-old little sister. By then, we had left D.C. and moved to Prince George's County, Maryland. Our schedule, during the school year, involved us visiting Daddy and our brother on alternating weekends or staying with my cousins in Landover or Cheverly, Maryland. My Mommy eventually got an apartment in Greenbelt, Maryland. My little sister and I were latch-key kids, in Greenbelt, while our big brother, who was ten or eleven years old at the time, stayed in Seabrook, Maryland, then moved to Lanham, Maryland with our Daddy. As time pressed on, we were reunited with our brother, and we lived with our mother.

Now, fast forwarding to one day in high school, during the Fall of my senior year. On this one particular day, a group of recruiters arrived on a hunt for some new recruits. By this time, we had relocated to Raleigh, North Carolina. Initially, I rejected the thought but began to pray about what I should do and spoke to my mother, maternal grandfather (Poppy), and my uncles. Most of them, for their own reasons, really did not want me to go into the military. I did not think too much of the situation, until the recruiters returned in the Spring, armed with persistent efforts to coax and convince me. I enlisted in the United States Army.

I was sold out and ready to protect, serve, and die if I had to for my country. Then, after enduring a physical training test and completing "remedial training", involving pushups and weight-lifting. I awoke the next morning feeling like something was strange. When I attempted to get out of my bunk, I realized that both of my hands were swollen, blue, and purple in color, and they had no feeling. My army buddy, squad members, and Drill Sergeants alike were all shocked and could not believe their eyes either. I was immediately sent to Sick Call. They ran several tests and ended up casting me. The interesting thing about it all is that the Drill Sergeant, who wanted me to serve in a leadership position, forced me and another soldier to "micromanage" another soldier in performing her personal hygiene and serve CQ (guard duty) while there was a Drill Sergeant knowingly fraternizing with other female soldiers. In addition, I had a weapon discharged over the top of my head in the barracks.

Through it all, I did my best to remain positive and I successfully completed and qualified in all the required training, except the pushups. Because of the injury to my hands, I could no longer do push-ups, and returned home. In hindsight, the military knew what they were doing to this African American teenager. They sold me a dream, failed to protect or provide reasonable care for me while enlisted, and did not even grant me a medical discharge, as they should have. So today, almost THIRTY YEARS later, I am still seeking my service-connected benefits, which they, to this day, continue to deny.

SAFE FROM THE WEAPONS FORMED

Despite all I went through as a child, summer was a time of awesomeness. During the summers, my brother, sister, and I would enjoy spending our summers in Louisburg, North Carolina with our grandparents and cousins. The time spent during the summers fostered bonds between us and our cousins, who were more like siblings.

Through it all, I am still alive, though scarred after having more than seven surgeries and many more treatments, injections, and therapy on my mind, feet, knees, hands, and back, I am still alive. There were times when I wondered if I had died during the time while I was in service would they, the United States Army, have properly compensated my family? When I returned home, I enrolled in school and tried to return to a sense of normalcy but ended up in an abusive relationship. I was seeking my ex-fiancé' to build me back up, to restore me, since the Army had broken me down. Instead, since I had been body shamed in Basic Training, being told one day, "Private, you are eating too much, you need to lose weight." Then, being told almost the very next week, "Private, you need to start eating and gain some weight." When I heard it from my ex-fiancé', it was familiar.

I misunderstood the verbal abuse; believing that it was care and concern. But it escalated to physical abuse; a smack, punch, or being pulled down the stairs by my hair. Then, there was the micromanagement of what I wore, where I went, how long I was gone, when, where, and if I wore lipstick. This was masqueraded as love. After all, he was the protector. When I realized what was happening, I was filled with shame and guilt, so I learned how to suck it up and keep going, smiling outside while I was crying inside. YET, through it all, it was God who kept me safe in His arms, shielding me from the weapons that were formed. Despite all that I was going through, I realized that I had to live to see another day because God had greater plans for me.

SURVIVOR

As someone who survived an abusive relationship, misrepresentation of the military's promises to provide for my college education, train, and equip me, and the abuse and misuse of my time, talents, gifts, love, and loyalty, I am still safe in His arms.

SAFE FROM ALL HURT, HARM, AND DANGER

With God keeping me, you... us safe from the ways and wilds of this world, through the precious gift of HIS only begotten SON, we cannot and will not succumb to evil. The Bible reminds us in the ninety-first Psalm (New Revised Standard Version):

1 You who live in the shelter of the Most High, who abide in the shadow of the Almighty,
2 will say to the Lord, "My refuge and my fortress; my God, in whom I trust."
3 For he will deliver you from the snare of the fowler and from the deadly pestilence.
4 he will cover you with his pinions, and under his wings, you will find refuge; his faithfulness is a shield and buckler.
5 You will not fear the terror of the night, or the arrow that flies by day,
6 or the pestilence that stalks in darkness, or the destruction that wastes at noonday.
7 A thousand may fall at your side, ten thousand at your right hand, but it will not come near you.
8 You will only look with your eyes and see the punishment of the wicked.
9 Because you have made the Lord your refuge, the Most High your dwelling place,
10 no evil shall befall you, no scourge come near your tent.
11 For he will command his angels concerning you to guard you in all your ways.
12 On their hands they will bear you up, so that you will not dash your foot against a stone.
13 You will tread on the lion and the adder, the young lion and the serpent you will trample under foot.

14 Those who love me, I will deliver; I will protect those who know my name.
15 When they call to me, I will answer them; I will be with them in trouble, I will rescue them and honor them.
16 With long life I will satisfy them and show them my salvation.

I now know and have fully surrendered to God's will for my life, and continue to grow in the understanding that all I have been through and will go through, including being:

- <u>*Sexually assaulted*</u> - He may have raped me, but God restored me!
- <u>*Suspected*</u> - Folks may have misperceived how I conceived my son, because I was a single mother with a son, not realizing I *had been* married to my son's father, was separated, and then divorced.
- <u>*Smeared*</u> - She may have attempted to convince people that I was after their husband because I was a single black female minister without a husband. She did not realize that, YES, I am a single black female minister. However, I am not, and was not, seeking a husband. I was serving while waiting for God to allow a husband to find me.

All of this has not killed me but shown me that I should not allow people's ignorance, jealousy, envy, or lack of understanding of the something special about me, cause me to swerve from the path God has chosen for me. It is all about God! Victory occurs through His saving grace which the sacrifice of His Son has provided for us, through faith, and HIS keeping and sustaining power.

SAVED BY GRACE

It is that same saving grace that is available to everyone, especially you! Please read, receive, understand, and believe this… YOU ARE SALVAGEABLE! It does not matter what you did, have done, or are doing right now in your life that may be displeasing to God. What matters is that you know, trust, and believe in God, His Son, and His redeeming and healing power.

Now, PAUSE and think back over your life, and all you have been through (good, bad, and indifferent).

I'll wait…

And YOU ARE STILL HERE! HALLELUJAH! This is what GOD wants you to grasp, and I want YOU to understand; though the enemy meant it all for evil, GOD meant it for YOUR GOOD! GOD LOVES YOU! You have been chosen and set apart! God is waiting for YOUR YES! God has a customized plan just for you and your life. God created you in His image; fearfully and wonderfully made you! He created you! He knows who you are better than you do. He knew there would be things that He had to allow you to do, go, be, become, remain in, and turn away from in order that you may return and receive the fullness of Him at an appointed time. God's plans for you are not of evil (Jeremiah 29:11)! God created you to *have dominion over the things in the sea, air, and on land…every creeping thing that creepeth upon the earth* (Genesis 1:26-28). God created each of us to worship Him! (Isaiah 43:21) Not only with our mouths, but with our hearts, life, and living, every day, and doing it *in spirit and in truth* (John 4:24).

You have only read a portion of my story; all has not been shared with you YET! However, it was necessary for what has been shared to be so that you may know, trust, and believe that you are not alone. You have not been shunned nor sidelined; but selected for a time such as this to receive this message! You can and will make it through with the love of God and the help of the Lord. You are a blessing to this world! DO NOT SETTLE for the lies the enemy has told or tries to tell you or the temptation he has presented or will present to you. YOU are worth it, worthy of all God has for you, and deserving of God's best; the *exceedingly abundantly* His word speaks of. If you would, please remind yourself each and every day that you can be safe in HIS arms if you are not already! Please remain hopeful! The Bible reminds us, in Hebrews 11:1, that "Now faith is the substance of things hoped for, the evidence of things not seen". You, me... we must keep hoping and believing!
SAFE IN HIS ARMS

If you are not sure that you have been saved, set free, and counted as safe in HIS arms, it costs you NOTHING but the time it takes to do it, for you to gain eternity. Do at least one of these things:

- **Romans 10:9-10-** Profess. "Declare with your mouth that Jesus is LORD, and God raised Him from the dead, and you shall be saved."
- **Acts: 16:31-** "Believe in the Lord Jesus, and you will be saved- you and your household."

That's it! Please begin studying your Bible and meditating on God's word. If you do not belong to a Bible-teaching church, please connect with one as soon as possible. And, whenever you feel weak or uncertain, remember you have changed the "S" on your chest to

SAFE IN HIS ARMS!

A Strategy to stay in the PRESS:

Pray

Rest

Believe with **E**xpectancy

Continue **S**peaking Intentionally What You Are Believing God For

And Always Remember That YOU ARE **S**afe In His Arms!

God loves you, and so do I, and there ain't nothing you can do about it!

Chapter 7

Dr. Mary McDougal-Heggie

Dr. Mary McDougal-Heggie

The Reverend Dr. Mary M. Heggie is an Associate Minister at New Providence Missionary Baptist Church, Fuquay Varina, North Carolina. She currently holds the office of Founder and CEO of the North Carolina Association for Women in Ministry, a nonprofit organization incorporated by state-wide chapters since 1984.

As a visionary, pioneer for women in ministry, author, conference speaker, preacher, and teacher, Dr. Mary Heggie was called into the ministry of Jesus Christ in 1984 and licensed to preach and ordained in 1985. She was the immediate former founder and pastor of the First Philadelphia Christian Center, Inc., Raleigh, North Carolina, a globalized, diverse, and multi-cultured church, from 2000-2016. After accepting God's call to return to full-time evangelism, empowerment, and global mission, Reverend Dr. Mary Heggie remains an active supporter of the Lott Carey Pastoral Excellence Program, the General Baptist State Convention, and the Raleigh Interdenominational Ministerial Alliance. She served as an Interviewer Representative for the Eastern Carolina Christian Seminary and Coordinator of Wake Missionary Baptist Association for Southern Area Churches while previously serving as Interim Pastor at her home church.

Many years ago, Dr. Heggie chose to take the road less traveled. Dr. Heggie's passions are expressed in her global ministry efforts to spread the liberating good news of the Gospel of Jesus Christ. She specifically directs her ministry works toward the people living in the most populated but least evangelized nations, which includes areas of Haiti, South America, the West Indies, and Europe. This has been and will continue to be the force behind her faithfulness to God's calling. Her early years of spiritual growth and maturity were influenced by the life, work and services of Mother Teresa of Calcutta.

Dr. Heggie authored her first book in 2011, entitled *We Refuse to Die Like This;* it has been used as a reference book for many women's bible studies and conferences. Her dissertation entitled, *"Missionary Perspectives in the Southern African American Churches,"* is also a modest celebration of the work and witness of great gifted global Christian leaders whose work has brought life-changing and life-giving hope to an untold number of people around the world.

Known as a trailblazer and having shattered the glass ceiling, Dr. Heggie was the 2009 Recipient of the Hannah Keith S.F., Inc. Award for Women of Influence by the Raleigh Human Relation/Faith in Action. She was a presenter on the George A. Crawley Women in Ministry Panel for the Annual Hampton University Minister's Conference in 2005. Dr. Heggie became an emerging voice at Dr. Susan Johnson's Women in Ministry International Conference in 2006-2008.

With an earned Doctoral Degree in Theology from Newburgh Theological Seminary, Reverend Dr. Mary Heggie holds a Bachelor of Arts Degree in Religious Studies from Meredith College, a Master of Arts Degree in Biblical Studies from Newburgh Theological Seminary, advanced graduate studies from Shaw University Divinity School and undergraduate studies in Business Administration at Shaw University. In December 2011, she received a prestigious Diploma in Pastoral Ministry from the Baptist Theological Seminary of Zimbabwe.

She is married and the proud mother of three adult children and four grandchildren. Her life's proverb is *"Let them look up and no longer see me but only You, Oh Lord!"*

To Connect with Dr. Heggie
Email: maryheggie7@gmail.com
Website: http://ncwomeninministry.com
Facebook: @NCAWM – The North Carolina Association for Women in Ministry

Trust the Process

"...because you have struggled with God and with humans and have overcome." Genesis 32:28b

It's a simple reminder that your divine destination is not what defines you...it's the process. It's the process that makes you. Having had my own struggles in life and after being in ministry for more than 40 years, I am certain of one thing and that is, it's the process that defines you. God takes His time. Our past can be brutal but necessary. And it becomes the waiting and the dance between waiting and patience.

I have attempted to describe in brief to the emerging generation of women in ministry how not to try to jump ahead of the process. In this chapter, I am sharing my bitterest defeats in life, how I have struggled with God and with humans and have prevailed. I believe that God wants to prepare us, equip us, and supply the right resources for our ministries. Moving ahead of God sometimes creates more struggles for us in the long run.

Often, people want the anointing and the blessing, but not the pain, the tears, the tests, and the trials. The cost of being tremendously used by God is extremely high, and there are many people who simply do not want to pay the price. There is a price to pay and a season to go through, but God has designed our lives so that the joys far outweigh the tears. We, as women of God, are sometimes guilty of doing all *the right things at the wrong time*. Therefore, we must be willing to trust the process.

Looking Back: I didn't see it coming!

"If I should die before I wake …Now I lay me down to sleep, I pray Thee Lord my soul to keep. If I should die before I wake, I pray Thee Lord my soul to take." This was the first prayer I ever learned as a child. A journey through thick darkness and prolonged nights illuminated the power in this prayer. In the midst of this journey into unknown regions of suffering, dark, murky, waters, and uncharted territory, God has an overriding purpose: The you that were seen become the Christ that is known!

I wasn't born a pastor, preacher, teacher, or an evangelist. I wasn't born becoming one of the first females ordained by an established Baptist association when women were not allowed to preach from the pulpit. I wasn't born chief executive officer for the North Carolina Association for Women in the Ministry. I wasn't born with an interest in advocating for women's rights or for human rights. Nor was I born to become president of what once was considered, a male-dominated Interdenominational Ministerial Alliance. I wasn't born a disciple of Jesus Christ or to travel internationally ministering to other nations. I certainly wasn't born to under shepherd one of God's beloved churches. I wasn't born a wife, mother, or grandmother.

My mother and grandmothers could never have imagined me living a life as a woman preacher. Nor could my Grandfather George have ever imagined it in his time, even as God allowed him to seed His Word into my spirit while sitting on the front porch of my mother's home.

I am amazed at how early in life the enemy was already at work trying to take my life. Raised later by a single parent, I remember my mama having to provide for five children after my father left home with her best friend. I was the oldest. My mom told me that when I was approximately three years old, I would walk around trying to sing a song by the Five Blind Boys of Alabama entitled, *"You'll Never Walk Alone."* With lyrics: *When you walk through the storm, hold your head up high. And don't be afraid of the dark.* Little did I know that the words of that song would one day carry me through some of the darkest times in my life! Can you imagine? Even then God had a purpose and plan for my life. A plan that not even my mother could have imagined when she gave birth to me.

Spiritual warfare is like a thread that runs in and through your life as you bring forth a ministry you never knew you were carrying. Disaster strikes; you never saw it coming. When we don't see something coming, it can be more than a mild disruption, and more than a catastrophe. It can be a long and slow decline. It can be deterioration and decay over weeks, months and even years. That may be the most dangerous thing not to see. A long, slow deterioration.

As I started on this paradoxical journey, I also carried secrets buried deep within me. Satan knew my past and he knew my past record. I was handicapped, maimed, and wounded. Even as I write this chapter, I am amazed at how God used my past to remind me of where I've been and where I should never want to return.

At the tender age of ten, I was raped by a white man. It happened one summer morning around 10:00 o'clock. This all happened in the late 50s during the time of great unrest between blacks and whites. The very fact that prejudice and racial injustice were engulfing the community created something of a waiting time bomb enraged with so much hatred and anger. I could have never known when this unpleasant incident happened. There would be a burst of anger and vengeance. I never knew the effect that day would have on the community, city, and church. I would never know, until later in life, of the impact that this experience would have on my life. Local newspapers were carrying the story… It was such a horrific time in my life that for so many years, I chose to block it from my mind rather than deal with it. It was a "hush, hush" in my family amongst the adults.

In my adult life, I had the symptoms of an unknown yet awful disease. It first appeared on my face. I had to wear a cover of makeup, which was to my distaste, and it caused others to stare and whisper about my condition. This systemic form of the disease involved other organs in my body. I went from doctor to doctor, and no one could diagnose the condition. It is a disease that will hide itself. Due to the stress, fatigue, aches and pains, rashes, hair loss, memory loss, and headaches, depression set in. The disease was later diagnosed as Lupus.

I knew I was dying spiritually, but I also felt as if I was dying physically. Lupus is the type of disease that contributes to the kind of depression that makes you go from here to there. It was as if I was all alone. My family didn't know. My marriage was in disarray. I wanted out. It was then that I tried to commit suicide, but God didn't let me succeed.

During this time in my life, I would experience spiritual warfare at night. The enemy would attack me in bed. It was severe. I would awake, at night, and this dark form would be over my bed trying to tie my legs or move up to my hands. Sometimes climbing over on top of me to try and kill me. Once, the struggle was so intense that the spirit said, "Don't let him get you to the floor, or you will die." Through these struggles, I would plead the blood of Jesus and call out the name of Jesus, and the dark form would go away. Ephesians 6:12 states "For we wrestle not against flesh and blood, but against principalities, against powers, against the rulers of the darkness of this world, against spiritual wickedness in high places."

I was still having dreams and visions. Three lions showed up on my bed one night. I was barely awake, but from my bed, I could see the light on in the bathroom, so I knew I was still in my bedroom. All three of the lions were brown and ferocious and all three came towards me, one right after the other. I was spiritually wrestling with each one. The largest one came first. It was horrible, but I got him down by wrestling with him while pleading the blood and calling out in my subconscious, the name of Jesus. Immediately, just as soon as the first lion went away, there came the second one. It was all I could do to hold him off as I repeated the same steps. Just as he disappeared the third one showed up. He wasn't as large as the second one, but he was hanging on to me by the sleeve of my pajamas with his teeth. I was getting tired and feeling very weak, but I knew I could not give up or give in. I had to keep fighting. I know that this was a vision. I don't know how long this struggle with the third lion went on, but finally, he disappeared. I became fully awake, sat up on my bed, and turned the nightstand lamp on. What did all this mean? It was a while before I could get myself together.

Several days later, the Spirit had me to turn to the book of Genesis, to the chapter where Jacob wrestled with a man until the breaking of day. After reading the chapter, one word stood out in my mind. Through the visions and the biblical story of Jacob, I believe the Spirit was revealing to me the word, "Prevailed." I believe that was one of the most significant turning points in my life. Could this have been an indication that the Lion of Judah was in my life and divinely moving me to a higher spiritual level in my life? One thing was certain; I had to fight for my life! I was in Peniel!

When the Past is Brutal but Necessary

Don't jump the process. Sometimes, life seems so unfair. I linger on this foundation because many who read this, are struggling against the "accuser." You are expecting payback. You think you are living under divine retribution. Like me, you may have suffered a divorce, marital abuse, rape, and thoughts of suicide. Your previous relationships may have consisted of an unfaithful spouse or an absent parent. You may have suffered great financial losses and bankruptcy, or you've been mocked and made fun of. Perhaps you have been publicly disgraced because of lies, betrayal, and rejection. And in your suffering, while you were down, the enemy, people, and your own thoughts were ganging up against you!! Your mind was telling you that God was "out to get you." Your past can be brutal.

It was then, almost immediately, while preaching, teaching, and facilitating many women's conferences on a wider platform, my life took a downward spiral again. My life seemed to be unraveling right before my eyes. I was helpless. Because of who I was in the eyes of the public, I couldn't tell anyone. Not even the many sisters whom I had counseled. What I failed to realize is that there is a process that God must walk you through.

I had to choose whether to become bitter or allow the situation to make me better. I had nothing but the promise of God to hold on to. Through all of that, God was merciful. He knew I was sick and needed help. And because of that very fact, God took care of me.

Later, in the Spring of 2005, five years into me planting my church, I flew to Los Angeles to attend an international women's conference. A half hour before the session was to open, the convener called me on the phone and asked if I could share my life story with those in attendance. She shared with me a dream she had of me the night before. We'd never been personable, so I was awestruck. I almost passed out! What? Share my life story? Reveal the deep, hidden secrets of my inner wounds and scars? Never in my whole life had I ever been asked to do that. In addition to being surprised, I was also very nervous about doing this and not really being prepared. This would be on an international platform, and I was stressed at the very thought of standing before thousands. What would I say? All my life I had suppressed my personal feelings. Now God was asking me to tell my story.

I knew that God was up to something. It was a divine setup! When I was introduced and invited to the podium, I began to talk about my life from childhood on into my adult life, and the power of God began to break up fallow ground. People were openly crying out loud! There were many of the sisters bending over in their seats trying to hide their pain, but the tears were flowing. Several of the sisters began running through the conference room crying out in agony as in a helpless state. That is when I knew my calling! The word of God clearly expressed to me that my ministry was healing, deliverance, and restoration!

God showed me my future ministry. During this time in my life, the Spirit of God led me to organize the North Carolina Association for Women in Ministry, Inc. I saw people damaged by broken relationships, pain, and despair; people stuck in a valley of hopelessness. It was not going to be enough to pat them on the head and say, "God will make a way somehow." I had to journey to the valley of hopelessness myself, set up camp there, and learn to survive.

I have never met a person who has not struggled with or suffered deep wounds because of a broken relationship. Whether this brokenness occurs in a dysfunctional family, from abuse, with the loss of a loved one, or in a failed relationship, all human pain has its genesis in human relationships. This is why a deep, sincere, abiding, and intimate relationship with God is so vital to our lives.

If God's not through working, I'm not through waiting!

God sometimes slows our progression down just enough to accommodate our hasty anxieties. He factored into His plan for our lives the times we entered seasons of fear and failed to trust Him. I'm not through waiting. I'm through fighting, I'm through wrestling. I yield myself over to God. It's not easy, its suffering, it's difficult. If God's not through working, I'm not through waiting. I had to trust the Process.

Less than two years after separation and divorce, God counseled me in my apartment for over two hours, and then, He said, "*Reconcile with your husband.*" My flesh wanted to resist that command, but God had made me to understand that He had principles and He had stipulations. Because He loved me so, He wanted me to go back to my husband. He said trust Me. Then the questions came as they were presented to Peter. "How much do you love me? If you go back, I'll be with you. I will never leave you nor forsake you."

I knew there would be shame, ridicule, and mockery. I had to forgive. Each of us has a choice in forgiving others of past mistakes and in this life, we will have many opportunities to forgive or not to forgive others. When we have the capacity to choose not to forgive others, we expose ourselves for not having faith in God's forgiveness towards us.

By this time, God's peace and love were surrounding me. I humbled myself with much humility. I gave up my life for His life in me. I made the decision that it "was no longer I who lived, but He who would live inside of me." I was willing to give it all up just to be with Him and so "that I may know Him and the power of His resurrection, and the fellowship of His sufferings, being conformed to His death" (Philippians 3).

Several years later, God again said to me, "I want you to tell your story." Write a book. I began to panic. I knew I was opening myself up to criticism and ridicule. My life would be an open sepulcher. How would it affect my family, my church family, and the few friends I had left? What impact would it have on the many women and men I had ministered to in the past? He said, "Whom the Son sets free is free indeed." Then He said, "I not only want you to tell it to the backslider and the new convert, but I want you to tell it to the religious sector, the spiritual leaders in the household of faith. I want you to tell it to those sitting in high places."

He said, "It's about accountability. I want you to bring this *spirit* to the nation. To join millions of servants who are out in the trenches." Then I saw myself, in a dream, hanging onto a rope from a plane that would take me to places I'd never dreamed about or had even thought of.

In 2011, I self-published my first book, *We Refuse to Die Like This!* It was through the writing of this book that I was healed, delivered, and set free!

Today I am preparing for what lies ahead. I don't know what the future holds, but *"I press toward the goal for the prize of the upward call of God in Christ Jesus"* (Phil 3:13-14). I've been strengthened and encouraged by the lives of so many people. But I would like to take this moment to thank people I've never met but whose lives have been a part of my transformation. I am waiting ... *"Until the Lord has given your brethren rest, as He gave you, and they also have taken possession of the land which the Lord your God is giving them..."* (Joshua 1:15). I cannot rest. You cannot rest. We cannot rest until the Lord has given all our brethren rest."

Closing Word and/or Tips on Trusting the Process:

The devil tries to divert our attention by using storms, trials, temptations, and tests. He wants to keep us from realizing our full potential in God. There are so many unsung songs, unwritten poems, and unpublished books in the cemetery. They lie there dead because some people died in their spiritual winter without realizing their full potential.

God chooses our time of blessing. He knows just when to bless us, where to bless us, and how to bless us. But then when we complete the course, He receives the glory!

God has a plan for you. Ask God to show you a new way to view the trial you are going through. Every difficult situation in your life is useful and necessary for your growth in God. Any kind of development requires a process. Your story is not over yet, He is bringing greater beauty and strength through every hard moment. God is able to carry you straight through. Just trust the process!

I had to write this chapter for you!

Chapter 8

Rev. Dr. Pamela Holder

Rev. Dr. Pamela Holder

For I reckon that the sufferings of this present time are not worthy to be compared with the glory which shall be revealed in us. Romans 8:18

Reverend Dr. Pamela Holder is a teacher, preacher, and singer upon whom God has poured out His Spirit to serve the present age.

Born in Queens County, New York, to the late Reverend Dr. Curtis M. Carrington, Sr. and the late Mrs. Shirley W. Carrington, Dr. Holder grew up in a musical environment, releasing several recordings with her family. They traveled locally and internationally to share the Gospel of Jesus Christ through music. In addition to singing, she studied violin.

On March 17, 2001, Dr. Holder preached her introductory sermon, "The Rock that Rocked the Jailhouse," and in 2003, she was ordained by the High Point Education and Missionary Baptist Association.

Since 2021, Dr. Holder has served as Pastor of Bethel "A" Baptist Church in Brevard, North Carolina. She was elected to the City Council of Brevard in 2023. In addition, she serves on the Executive Board for *Rise and Shine,* an afterschool tutoring program offered at Bethel A, the Board of Directors for S.A.F.E. of Transylvania County, a domestic violence and sexual assault agency, The Brevard/Transylvania County Housing Coalition, and she is 1st Vice President of the NAACP of Transylvania County.

Prior to her assignment as pastor, Dr. Holder worked as a Chaplain at Cone Health for 17 years and taught middle and high school English/Literature and Speech.

In addition to undergraduate studies and earning her Master's and Doctor of Divinity degrees, she completed 10 years of Bible Study Fellowship International.

She is a proud mother of one daughter of Atlanta, a grandmother, and sister of one surviving brother of Atlanta. She considers family to be her greatest earthly blessing.

Dr. Holder has ministered through preaching, singing, and presenting workshops, locally and internationally. In all that she does, Dr. Holders's primary goal in life is to influence others to pursue a personal relationship with God through salvation in Jesus Christ.

A woman of excellence, she believes all things should be done decently and in order. 1 Corinthians 14:40.

Dr. Pamela Holder
pchpreacher@yahoo.com

From the Pit to the Pulpit

The Carrington Family formed when my mom and dad met and were married in Queens, New York. My dad was an R&B recording songwriter, vocalist, and pianist. Following one of his concerts in New York he told his band members that the Lord told him to make that his last night. He said his drummer told him he needed another drink and, refusing another drink, he reiterated it was his last night in the club and singing R&B. Shortly after that announcement, he moved the family to North Carolina, bringing us closer to my mother's family.

My father was adopted by a family in Virginia where he grew up. His father was a deacon and his mother an usher, but more importantly, they loved the Lord and raised all four of their adopted children in a Christian home. Daddy was a self-taught musician and played for several churches until God called him to preach. After he was licensed and ordained, he planted a church that flourished for over forty years.

I am the only daughter of four children and yes, my brothers teased me, frequently. However, they always had my back whenever outsiders bothered me. After we moved to North Carolina, my dad taught my brothers and me to sing Gospel music and he started his own record label and recorded several other artists. We traveled up and down the east coast and even to Nassau and Freeport, Bahamas singing concerts and selling our recordings.

In addition to singing, my dad kept a secular job and when he started preaching and pastoring his church, he was frequently called to preach revivals and special services. I was always interested in his preaching and pastoral work and usually traveled with him. I remember, even in high school, titles of sermons would come to mind during everyday activities. Of course, I ignored them because, women didn't preach!

My aunt was the first woman preacher that I knew. Since my dad would have her preach for him, I was introduced to the idea of a woman preacher. However, she and I were quite different. I was shy; she was not. I could sing and enjoyed doing that, but she did not. I was quite shy (as a child) and very conservative. The fact that my dad supported her as a woman, gave me hope, but I didn't feel called and didn't quite understand what "called" meant or looked like.

As I fast-forward, I went the scenic route to college after getting married, six months after my high school graduation, and later divorced when my daughter was almost three years old. My brother said I married to get out of the house. We will talk more about that later. It was hard, as a single parent, to take college courses, and work full-time. I always knew there was more for me to do, but I didn't know what.

I married a second time, but seven months into that marriage he began physically abusing me. I was devastated and embarrassed. I left less than three years into the marriage while living in Columbia, South Carolina. It took me that long because it was my second marriage! My parents and grandparents stayed together. That was all I knew!

After research and job searches, I moved to Charlotte, North Carolina and joined Bible Study Fellowship International and attended for over 10 years. About five years in, I was married to a pastor. I had prayed for a life/ministry husband who was saved. The night we met, the Lord clearly told me, "You are going to meet your husband tonight" and I did. A few years later, my dad was diagnosed with Parkinson's Disease and had to retire from his ministry as Pastor. He asked my husband to pray to succeed him. After a year of praying, my husband resigned from the church he was pastoring, and we moved from Charlotte to Greensboro.

For me, the idea of preaching was overshadowed by adjusting to my role as a pastor's wife and what that would look like since my parents were still active in the ministry. I really didn't want to overshadow my mother's role.

I continued with Bible Study Fellowship International – since it is a worldwide study, they had a fellowship in Greensboro. Despite the distractions, I could not dismiss the idea that was becoming more apparent, that I knew I was supposed to preach. The Lord had given me the sermon title and scripture. Still, I was afraid to say anything. After all, I was not like other women, and who would dare think of a woman preaching in a man's world? I started getting physically ill and had several hospital emergency department visits with debilitating abdominal cramps. The Lord clearly said during one of those visits, "You need to birth what is in you."

I finally gained the courage to talk with my husband about what I was experiencing. I once asked him how does one know when they're called to preach and he said, "If you can do anything else, do that." I was at the point where I couldn't do anything else.

When I had the "I've been called to preach" talk with my husband, he was excited, which surprised me. I thought he would give reasons why I should not, but I had his support. Next, I knew I needed to talk with my dad. I had already decided to go to a bible college or seminary for academic support and to continue Bible Study Fellowship. So, I told my dad I was going back to school because I was ready to answer the call to preach. As though we had the conversation yesterday, I remember his face and how it was lit with joy. It was as though he knew, but never told me. He said to me, "It's going to be hard for you because you're a woman, but you're strong, and you can do it."

The PIT – The *Public*

As a "preacher's kid" and gospel recording family, it seems we were always in the public spotlight. People knew my dad so well that when I was pulled over for speeding, the officer knew my family name and asked if I was Curtis Carrington's daughter.

What the public didn't see were the inner workings of our home. My mother had suffered a nervous breakdown in her teens. In retrospect, I believe her illness was never properly treated. She catered to the boys, and as the only girl, I felt rejected. That's why my brother told me I married early to leave home.

As I grew older, and after my daughter was born, my mother and I bonded. However, due to a disagreement, we became estranged again, and at times it was not pretty. I grieved for her. My way of coping was through counseling, seeing a psychologist, and, at one point, a psychiatrist. I invited my mother and my dad to attend a session with me, but she refused.

Shortly after my talk with my dad about my call to preach, he transitioned to be with the Lord due to injuries from a car accident. He died at the scene. As the public watched the news coverage that Dr. Curtis Carrington, Sr., a pastor and recording artist died in a car accident and respectfully said their goodbyes, I had to say goodbye to "daddy." During my complicated grief, the Lord clearly told me, "Your earthly father introduced you to your Heavenly Father to take care of you when he was here and when he transitioned."

After the homegoing of my dad and a period of mourning, I shared with my mother that God was calling me to preach. However, her reaction was vastly different than my dad's. I still remember the sound of the door slamming behind me as I walked to my car.

The public noticed her absence at my initial sermon and doctoral commencement. The public also watched as my family went through a church split; the same church to which my father had asked my husband to succeed him. Although the events were years apart, the public watched.

Years after my father's death, I faced another blow. After more than 25 years of marriage, I had to accept the fact that it was over. Shortly after the separation, my mother and I became estranged, again. I had layers of grief for my father (which resurfaced), and now I grieved the loss of my husband and my mother. I had my moments of anger, denial, blame, fear, anxiety, and even a moment of questioning my presence, my purpose, and life itself.

The public watched as I continued to work as a clinical care chaplain and teach full-time. They watched as I navigated through my life, laced with rumors and false narratives. The public watched, but from a distance, since we were in COVID and sheltered in place. I often wondered how this happened to me! I would listen to myself in counseling sessions and think, had I not lived this life that I was speaking about, I would have a tough time believing it.

The PIT – The *Internalizing*

Everything became too much, and I began to isolate and internalize. My therapist helped me understand my reactions to toxic relationships, but it still did not take away the pain of rejection, abandonment, my misrepresented character, the deep sadness, and the intense loneliness. I questioned God and quit believing in myself. I searched for strength by watching worship services on YouTube. In all that I was going through, I didn't want to let go of God, but I didn't understand Him either.

The internalization began spilling over into my counseling sessions, and soon, I was no longer interested in continuing. There had to be another way. My three-year-old grandson would often tell me, "Mama God's got you." I had not shared my journey with him, but God knew how to use my grandson to encourage me. I shared little with my daughter, and for a long time, I didn't tell my only surviving brother. Internalizing felt safe. It even felt believable that if I internalized, I wouldn't have to face the fear of the unknown.

One morning, I was crying as I was driving to school to teach. The Lord grabbed my attention and said, "Listen." CeCe Winans was singing, "He's Concerned About You" on Sirius. I sat in the parking lot of the school and sobbed. Yes, the public had seen a snapshot of my life, but God had seen it all. Just knowing He was concerned about all that was public, private, and internalized, gave me hope.

The PIT – The *Transitions*

During the transition of my life to constant new normalcies, there was also a restoration of the relationship between my mother and me. I had been preaching for several years before she came to support me. But that was not as important as the fact that on a few occasions she was there. In fact, on a couple occasions she introduced me. I was so proud of her.

I finally began talking to my daughter and a couple of close friends about what I was feeling, facing, and my fear of the unknown. My immediate family and friends helped me transition in ways that I could not have faced alone.

Being in the pit was dark. I didn't see my way in, and I certainly couldn't see my way out of it. It seemed, at one point, I was going from one pit to another. Each one darker, lonelier, and, like an oven pit, even hotter. The pit was an extremely unpleasant and depressing place. The conditions of the pit were the absolute worst.

Praise God, I didn't stay in the pit. God delivered me out of the pit and placed me in the pulpit. The pulpit is a place of an elevated platform or high reading desk used in preaching or conducting a worship service. That is the first definition. The second definition is that it is the preaching profession.

However, I can best relate to the third definition. The pulpit is a preaching *position*.

Before the foundation of the world, and before my parents ever met, God *positioned* me to preach. While I was in each pit, God was preparing me to *position* me to preach the Gospel. The public's eye, opinion, and judgment were meant to *position* me. The internalization and isolation *positioned* me. The transition from one pit to the next was to *position* me, rather than give me a position.

My call to preach was challenged by some but supported by many. I had to remember the latter rather than dwell on the first. I admit, I was fortunate to get some invitations because of the respect and character of my dad. He told me it would be hard because I am a woman. But because of who he was and who God is, as a woman preacher, it was easier for me than some. Most of the resistance came from family. Of the few times my calling was challenged, I remember one pastor told me I would not be invited into his pulpit. Quite frankly, I was okay with his decision. I know who I am whether I am in the pulpit or the bathroom.

A few months later, he invited me to preach for his 11:00 service, Women's Day of course, but I was grateful. He said he had been watching me and that I would be the first woman to preach for him. He was proof that the public was watching how I carried myself.

One of the most difficult transitions was from marriage to divorce. For the first time, I understood why God hates divorce. A loving Father would not want His child to hurt so deeply. As I transitioned from married to divorced, a two-income home to one income, and the dream of physical death to part us to the death of a marriage, I felt lost. I had been down the aisle three times but married only once.

Turning FROM the Old and Turning TO the New

My brother told me that if I would let go (of my past) and let God, He could take me to where He wanted me to be. So, I let go and let God! I received a call from a dear friend asking if I could preach one Sunday for a congregation that did not have a pastor. Since we were still in COVID, I had to submit my sermon via a Zoom recording, which they posted for the Sunday morning service. Later, I received a call asking if I would be interested in submitting my bio and resume for consideration. I did, and later, they asked for a live recording that I had preached and for references.

Well, I began doubting myself. I googled the church and learned it was 102 years old and had never had a female pastor. Not only am I a female, but I was also separated, at the time, and facing a divorce. I was sure they would not select me!

However, I submitted all they requested, and one day, I received a call asking for an interview. They wanted me to interview, teach Sunday School, and preach the 11:00 worship service. I had been praying since I got the call to submit my resume, but I also internalized it. I didn't want to tell people in case it ended in disappointment. However, my references, including one of my best friends, called me. The search committee was inquiring.

At the close of my interview weekend and visit, I knew I was in love with the congregation. They asked tough questions, opened their arms, and when it was time to go, they prayed for me. Several said, "You'll be back." Of course, I knew there was a process. I prayed that whatever decision they made, especially if it were for me to pastor the congregation, would be a unanimous vote. I didn't want to go to a congregation that was divided about their decision of who would be their pastor. Later I learned that the vote was unanimous. I have been serving as Senior Pastor of Bethel A Baptist Church in Brevard, North Carolina since 2021. Praise God!

Little did I know that I would transition from pains that often landed hard in the pit of my stomach, to pastor a church. That three-year-old grandson is seven now, and although he would frequently say, "Mama, God's got you", he does not say it now. Somehow, he knows I have transitioned from loss to gain, from pain to promise, and from the pit to the pulpit.

Despite the hardships, I praise God for each pit. It is my bridge to my purpose and position. It is my inspiration to inspire others. It is how God used each one for His glory to teach me that I may teach others. Coming out of the pit, I realized the answer to my question, "How can a woman preach in a man's world." With God, not only can a woman preach in a man's world, but she can also pastor.

I'm reminded of the hymn, "Hold to God's Unchanging Hand", by Jennie Bain Wilson. I am proof that life is *FILLED with swift transitions; naught of earth unmoved can stand.* That's why we must *build our hopes on things eternal and hold to God's unchanging hand.*

The second verse has been proven to me time and time again. It says, *trust in Him, who will not leave you; whatsoever the years may bring; when your earthly friends forsake you; still more closely to Him cling.* I have learned to cling to God and hold to His unchanging hand. By holding to His hand, He transitioned me, indeed grew me, from the pit to the pulpit.

Chapter 9

Rev. Marlo McCloud

Rev. Marlo McCloud

Born January 20th, 1970, in Philadelphia, Pennsylvania. Minister Marlo McCloud is the daughter of Deacon Thomas Statham and his wife, Denise, and Lois Rice-Robinson, and her husband, Arthor Robinson Sr.

At the age of nine, she received the Lord Jesus Christ during a street ministry service, but she did not come to know him until the divorce of her parents. Her father, broken, went to a church with a friend and gave his life to the Lord. The name of the church is Celestial Zion Baptist Church where Marlo followed him and joined the church under the leadership of Rev. Dr. E. Boyd-Williams in 1982.

Minister Marlo McCloud graduated from Thomas Edison High School in Philadelphia, Pennsylvania. She went on to receive her nursing assistant certification, after which she attended Main Bible Institute and the Manna Bible College, receiving certificates of completion. Minister Marlo continued her education at Temple University Hospital of Philadelphia, Pennsylvania. Minister Marlo attended CITE School of Business where he received her diploma.

In 1992 Marlo received an honorary recognition from her church and Pastor E. Boyd-Williams for her dedication and loyal service. In 2000 Marlo received her ministerial license. Minister Marlo went on to become one of the leading ministers, President of the Usher Board, Facilitator of the New Member's Class, and Youth Sunday School Teacher.

Marlo was given a covenant word, Psalms 121. Minister Marlo became one of the associate ministers, conducting intercessory ministry, prayer ministry, and pastoral care ministry at Macedonia New Life Church, in Raleigh, North Carolina, under the leadership of Reverend Dr. Joe L. Stevenson. Marlo has attended the Heritage School of Biblical and Theological Studies under Dean and Instructor Rev. Ray Mayotte at Macedonia New Life Church. She successfully completed the in-service training course for Christian Theology and Church Polity in the fall of 2018. She is now called Reverend Marlo McCloud.

She is the mother of two awesome sons, Martel and Titus McCloud, and the grandmother of one handsome young man, Maxwyll McCloud. She is the sister to Thomas Rice, Arthor Jr., Mark Robinson, John and Nathaniel Williams, Karen Hunter who passed away and Danielle Statham and Erica Williams.

Reverend Marlo McCloud is a praise and worship leader and when the Holy Spirit is moving, she will dance if you don't watch out!

Challenges, Instructions & Guidance

Born and raised in the city of Philadelphia. I went to church on and off with my parents, my late grandmother, and my late Aunt Sue. My Aunt Sue would make sure that when we were with her or at home, she would say, "Make sure you come to church."

Coming to church was not one of my challenges; it was being asked to do things when I was there. My first pastor was a female, and she started her church in her home and then opened up a storefront church, right in the middle of Germantown Avenue. There was a church across the street, a church on the corner on your left, a big church with its own cemetery on your right, and around the corner, two more churches that were all run by male pastors. I could never remember the name of the church, I would just say, "That's Pastor Dunlap's church."

When going to church with my aunt, she would say, "Each one of you would have to testify of the goodness of the Lord." This church only had my aunt, Pastor Dunlap, neighborhood children, my cousins, and myself. This is where it started. The late Pastor Dunlap would say to me at age nine, "You will open up with a testimony and sing a song." "Testimony, and a song! I would say, "Why me, Pastor? When you have people here that are older than me." She would say to me, "I need you to say something, and sing something that will have everyone participating." So, the first thing that I did was pray, and then I would hear and feel something saying to me, "Tell them the story about when you were in the hospital with asthma. Tell them about your dad walking in a snowstorm, because someone stole his car, and there were no buses running and no cab to come get you." Then I would start singing- "Yes, Jesus Loves Me for the Bible Tells Me So". Each Sunday the Lord would give me a new testimony and a new song. I would always look at Pastor, Aunt Sue, and my cousins to see if I did okay. My cousins would look back at me and smile because they knew Pastor and my aunt would not be calling on them any time soon. This is when the Lord helped me with my challenge of speaking. He instructed me on what to say and then guided me through it all.

When I think back to the 1970's, Pastor Dunlap was one of the female preachers who had to start her own church. She would say that you would have to wait for the male pastor or preacher to recognize you. When her Pastor would come to visit, he would call her, Sister Dunlap, and he would go up in the pulpit, and she would come down and sit with us. I never understood why until later in my teenage years.

When it came to school, it was so different from church. In church, it was family and friends, and no one was laughing or making me feel bad. I heard the word of God saying to me Psalms. 138:8 -"*The Lord will perfect that which concerns me,*" because they knew Pastor would not be calling on them. Knowing what God did and knowing what God said to me helped me with speaking in the church. In school, I had a favorite elementary school teacher, the late Ms. Washington. She knew my favorite place in the classroom was in the back. I tried not to be seen and not heard. I knew that she would have me put on my glasses and sit in the front of the room. I would shake my head and hear the kids in the room laughing and saying, "She's the teacher's pet!" Ms. Washington would say to me, "I need you in the front of the class not in the back." She believed that it was my eyes that were making it hard for me to read, see, and understand what was on the board. She always asked me to be the helper, to stay after class, and to stay after school so that we could practice reading, sounding out words, and writing for the next day of class. She would always say to me, "Practice reading out loud, practice writing so that you will stop all that erasing." I had a habit of using the wrong words in sentences.

Then she would say to me, "Breathe after every comma and period before starting the next sentence."

When it was lunchtime, she would send me to Mrs. Baker. She would also have me work on speaking by telling her about my day. I would say "Good", and she would say tell me in a sentence. I would take a deep breath and say, "My day is going good," and then she would tell me to tell her in a complete sentence how my day was going, and I would take another deep breath and say, "I am having a very good day today." She would laugh because I was taking deep breaths.

Ms. Washington spoke with my mother and said that I needed Mrs. Baker, "She will help Marlo until Junior High School." At the age of ten, I asked Mrs. Baker over and over again, "Why do I need to come to you when I have Ms. Washington?" She told me that she was a speech therapist and that I needed to come to her every day after lunch so that she could help me. With my head down, I prayed to the Lord, asking, "What's wrong with me?" Then Mrs. Baker said to me, "You are special to me and Ms. Washington." Both teachers had a meeting with my mom and said, "Your daughter has a learning disorder. This means that she will have to practice reading, writing, and speaking openly and not to herself. This will help Marlo with confidence when it comes to school and public speaking." Ms. Washington passed after I transferred to middle school. I still had Mrs. Baker; she became my English teacher and that's when she learned that I had Dyslexia. My disorder was due to problems identifying speech sounds, and learning how they relate to letters and words. I learned the meaning of Dyslexia: It's a result of individual differences in areas of the brain that process language (Webster). From middle school to junior high school, I had Mrs. Baker as my English teacher and speech therapist. She would laugh at me when I would practice and would breathe after every punctuation mark, and how I would smile after a book was read. You see, the Lord sent help with the challenges, gave me instructions, and guided me on to high school.

Moving Forward:

In high school, I started going to tutoring classes. In class, I felt good about myself because I was the first one to ask to read and to stand up and tell the class all about the book that I just read. I laughed to myself as I pictured my speech therapist laughing as I took deep breaths when reading and speaking; also knowing that I practiced for two days before (smiling on the inside)!

Now, I'm feeling confident about school and knowing all that I would have to do is practice, pray, and trust the ones that God has placed in my path.

Through middle school and high school, my parents were going through a breakup and divorce. I was the middle child, and the one that my siblings looked up to, and my parents included in the decisions that needed to be made. My siblings were asking, "What are we going to do?" My parents were asking, "Who do you want to stay with?" I was just trying not to be sick! I would remember what I had been taught by the late Pastor Dunlap. She would say to me, "God hears, and he already knows all about you."

I was the one who did not want to leave my dad alone. My siblings were waiting for me to tell them what we were going to do. So, I started praying, and asking, "Why my family, Lord?" I started crying; this was hard for me. In the middle of my cry, I heard the spirit, I smelled a beautiful fragrance, and I felt the presence of the Lord in the room with me, giving me peace. We stayed with my mother. It was hard for my mother because sometimes there was a shortage of food, and my mom would say to me, "We need just a few things." I was trying to keep my mind on doing well in school, not letting anyone know what I was feeling, and trying to be strong for my siblings and both of my parents. When my mother asked me to help, I would say, "Okay Mommy." Then, I would ask the neighbors if I could babysit for them, and I would ask our elderly neighbors if I could go to the store for them. For my babysitting, I would get $30 dollars, and for going to the store, sometimes it would be three dollars or five dollars. I would give that to help my mother and to help feed my siblings. One day, I prayed, asking God how I could help, and I heard the spirit of the Lord say, "Take a walk to your dad's house." As I was walking, I found a book of food stamps and a twenty-dollar bill. That's when I realized that my prayers work.

Back in the day, Value Plus and Murray's Meat Market were stores where we could shop and buy food and products all under twenty dollars. As I earned money, I would give it all to Mom, and then she would give me some back so that I could buy shoes at Value Plus that only cost two to three dollars, like Bobos, Laverne and Shirley's, and Jelly Beans (laughing). I would say to my mom, "Don't worry about me; get what you need for the family."

I was learning that prayer works and that after asking, there were instructions; the Lord would tell me where to go or who to talk to. Often, that would be both of my grandparents that the Lord would use. One giving me the spiritual side, and the other making sure that I kept up with my schoolwork. My father's mother was always making sure that the whole family came together on Sundays after church for dinner. She would say, "Pray for your dad and make sure that you go see him." My mother's mother would make sure that, when I broke my left arm, I could write with my right hand. She made sure that if I could repeat and sing those TV commercial songs, I needed to know my homework just like that. I would say to her, "Gramps, I'm strong in math, but in English I have challenges." She would say to me when I was with her, to go and get a book off her bookshelf and practice reading out loud.

The Lord Guiding Me:

Now my parents are divorced, and my dad is saying to God, "You cannot fix my broken heart." Again, someone had stolen his car, and as he went looking for it, he ran into one of his coworkers on her way to bible study, and she said, "Come go with me to church." My dad, with tears in his eyes, his job closing, and with very little money in his pockets, went. He met the woman of God that had changed his life and ours. She was very tall, and her name was, Pastor E. Boyd Williams. She had started the church in her home, then moved to renting buildings, and having her own church, called the Celestial Zion Baptist Church. When my dad joined, I followed him. I thought that it was just to support him. I started attending, thinking to myself, this is just to support, not to join. I watched my dad crying, and the Pastor saying, "Come to your father's side." My dad's coworker took me by the hand, walking me to the front of the church, and that was the day I joined the church. I was still torn between my parents, and I had to know that this was where God wanted me. My siblings and I got baptized, both of my parents remarried.

Growing up in Celestial Zion, I learned that Pastor had been a nurse to her Pastor. He was the pastor of the Corner Stone Baptist Church. She held many roles within the Women Conferences and became the first woman to be president of one of the Philadelphia Conferences. She began to train me, and we started with learning 12 scriptures weekly, making sure that I had them memorized. Then, Pastor moved on to having me by her side doing the communion and starting the service every Sunday morning with a song and opening up testimony service.

My Pastor continued to help me with my work in the ministry, and kindly encouraged me to practice writing sermons to preach every now and then to help with public speaking. Then she would say to me, "You will need to go to school." Shaking my head, I would respond, "Who me?" I started praying and praying some more. I started with going to a church of one of the Pastors that my Pastor recommended. Pastor Daniel's Institute was a beginning, and that's where I learned the words *exegesis* and *eisegeses* because he felt that I could not create a sermon using both words. He stated that I would not be preaching in anyone's church and that my pastor would have to work harder with me before sending me out to preach. He further explained that I would need extra help when going to school. I know that it was because of my dyslexia; putting together sermons would be a challenge. My Pastor worked diligently with me. First, she had me attend Main Bible Institute. Then she had me go to Manor Bible College for some courses. She was so proud to see that I did receive certifications of completion. Then I went to Temple University for some courses in business and medical billing, and then I received my certification and diploma at CITE School of Business. Even at these schools and the university, my challenges with dyslexia did not stop me from practicing and breathing. This is where my praises of thanksgiving come from.

I realized that I was called to the ministry when my children were born. I was very sick with both pregnancies. with my first son, I was told that I had toxemia; another term for pre-eclampsia. It was a very high-risk pregnancy. With my second son, I was told to put my feet up to abort him, due to tumors growing along with him. The doctors predicted that he would be stillborn or have some kind of birth defect. In each situation, my challenge was to hold on to my unborn child by following the instructions and guidance coming from God saying not so! I had to hold on to what my teachers had told me, what both Pastors had shown and taught me, and most of all, what the word of God said in Psalms 121, "*I will look to the hills from whence cometh my help*".

One day, I heard the spirit say to me, "I will make these words come to life by taking you through it, by demonstrating what was in the scriptures to you, and by instructing and guiding you. So, one holiday in the summer I was given a covenant word from the Lord: Psalms 121. I heard the spirit of the Lord say, "Take a trip with you and your sons and nephews to the Wild Wood, New Jersey beach. I said, "Lord, I don't know how to drive there on my own." So, I asked my then-husband to go with us, and he said, "No, I will be watching the game." I heard the spirit say, "Pack up and go." Back in those days, we had Map Quest. That meant you had someone reading the directions as you were driving. So, I had to do both; this was a challenge. I knew that the Lord was instructing me to follow that car and only look at the directions twice for my exit. When we arrived at the beach it was hot, the sun was beaming, and there was no shade anywhere. There was a gentleman with umbrellas, and he said to me, "Would you like an umbrella?" I said, "I don't have money". He said, "That's not what I asked you. Do you want an umbrella?" and I said, "Yes." Then, I heard the scripture again, "*That the Lord watches over you. The Lord is the shade at your right hand; the sun will not harm you by day.*" The man positioned the umbrella so that the shade would always cover me while I was on the beach. I saw the scripture become real to me, even that night, as we were trying to return home, "*The sun shall not smite thee by day, nor the moon by night. The Lord will keep you from all harm, he will watch over your life, you're coming and going*"; and we got home safely.

My then-husband moved us to North Carolina, and we joined Macedonia New Life under the leadership of Rev. Dr. Joe L. Stevenson, the first male pastor for us to be under his guidance. Aunt Macine and Aunt Erline, who passed away, were also members. Going through a divorce and having my then-husband still attending along with his girlfriend was another challenge. I said to myself, "I'm out of here. I will go back home", and I called my mom and said, "I'm coming back home." She said to me, "God has you there for a reason; you stay." Then I called my dad, and he said, "That Pastor there is your father; go to him." So, as I started walking to Pastor and First Lady Stevenson to tell him my plan, there was a member who stopped me. She said, "The Lord brought your face to me, and I want to know do you want to go to school." I looked at her and said, "I would like to, but I'm going to talk to the Pastor right now." Then she said to me, "The Lord told me to ask you because I was led to you to help you with going to school." I said, "Okay, I am going to speak with Pastor, and I will call you."

When I came to the Pastor, he stated to me that the church was starting a school within the church called the Heritage School of Biblical & Theological Studies. I began to laugh, shaking my head, and going back to that member to tell her that there will be a school starting up to help those who cannot afford to go to college, and one can gain course credits for attending this school. She stated to me that she would be my sponsor and would cover my expenses through the four years that it would take for me to finish! Then in the middle of all that, I got very sick and was hospitalized for a month. I had the most amazing professor who understood what I was going through and supported me in completing my coursework. My Pastor encouraged me by stating to me, "Marlo, you are no longer that lonely leaf on the tree. You are proving that with the help of the Lord, you can come through your challenges."

What the devil meant for evil; God meant it all for my good. I went from being a Minister to becoming Reverend Marlo McCloud. This is why I praise God so loud, and he gave me a holler and a dance. God did not stop there; he had my First Lady come to me and ask, "Are you ready to buy a home." My credit was another challenge, but God placed a beautiful person in my life, Ms. LaTreya, who helped me as I got my files, books, and needed materials together. That's what having dyslexia helped me to do; organize and have things in my life in order. Within three months after Pastor prayed over my book. Ms. LaTreya said to me, "You can go to the bank now." I went and I was approved! Full of excitement, I called First Lady and said, "Can we go look now?" God gave me a vision and told me to go look for a house with brick on the front and vinyl on the side. I was approved for only $100 thousand and was told that I would only be able to get a trailer house. Then I said to First Lady as we were looking at homes what the spirit of the Lord said to me. As we were riding, we drove right by the houses that had brick on them. First Lady stated, "We need to stay within the budget." So, everywhere we looked, there was no house that I liked. Then First Lady checked the real estate listings, and there was a house that had just popped up, and it was five minutes away. We started driving full circle to come to the same brick homes that the spirit of the Lord had shown me. To God be the Glory! I'm still living in that home. God will help you with your challenges, instruct you on how you can get it done, and guide you through it all!

In The End:

I learned that there are some Hollywood celebrities that had the same challenges that I had. Tiffany Haddish wrote a book about a special teacher who helped her with reading challenges. Fantasia Barrino also wrote a book about a special person in her life helping her with reading challenges, and there are so many more who have gone on to be great in this world. I was watching a TV show called "The Resident". In the show, each new resident had their own challenges, but there was one who wanted to become an Operating Room (OR) doctor. She had to work harder than the other residents in the hospital and was always seen drawing pictures of the human body to pass medical school classes and tests. She repeatedly practiced operating on cadavers, and she would practice committing all that she learned to memory. The part I believe about this show is that God wanted me to see that she had dyslexia but became a great OR surgeon. Even thou her family was ashamed of her disorder, she used it as her strength.

God will give you confidence. God will make you stand out when you want to fall back. God will perfect that which concerns you, whether it's reading, writing, speaking, or some other obstacle. He already has people or solutions designated to send your way to get you through all those challenges. God will empower the meek, and he will make beauty out of ashes. Know this, "you can lift up your eyes to the hills from whence cometh your help. Your help comes from the Lord". He knows your needs and will never leave you alone.

Remember always trust God for some things outside the box.

SALUTING BLACK WOMEN PREACHERS WHO LIVED THE CALL

The biographical sketches are quoted directly from Candice Benbow's article, "Black women preachers who changed-and are changing-history" (Benbow, 2022). They each reflect historical witness of the resilience and current expression of a courage that must be fueled by the Holy Sprit's power and presence.

Pauli Murray (1910-1985) - In 1977, Pauli Murray became the first African-American woman to be ordained a priest in the Episcopal Church. An activist and attorney, Murray coined the term "Jane Crow" in 1947 to highlight the racial and gender oppression Black women experienced during and post-Reconstruction. A queer person of faith, many scholars have begun to recognize Murray as one of the first transgender ministers. Murray's autobiography, "Song in a Weary Throat: Memoir of an American Pilgrimage," recounts a childhood in North Carolina and the experiences that formed a life of activism.

Prathia Hall (1940-2002) - A womanist, theologian, and ethicist, Rev. Dr. Prathia Hall is largely considered one of the greatest preachers of all time. During the Civil Rights Movement, she was an active member of the Student Nonviolent Coordinating Committee (SNCC) and is the inspiration behind Dr. Martin Luther King, Jr.'s famous speech, "I Have a Dream". Dr. Courtney Pace's, "Freedom Faith: The Womanist Vision of Prathia Hall" examines the life of one of the first women to be ordained in the American Baptist Churches, USA denomination. Additionally, Pace recently released an edited volume of Hall's sermons and scholarly essays.

Chapter 10

Rev. Yolande Murphy

Rev. Yolande Murphy

Reverend Yolande Murphy is the founder of Arisen Ministries in Raleigh, North Carolina. Founded in 2023, Arisen Ministries' mission is to aid people in arising from life's greatest challenges through Biblical teaching, Biblical preaching, Biblical Christian service, and Biblical life application by the Word of God.

Reverend Yolande was first licensed as a Minister of the Gospel in 2011, served as an Associate Minister and Pastor of Evangelism Ministry for 12 years, at Macedonia New Life Church, Raleigh, North Carolina. She was ordained for Ministry in 2021, all under the leadership of Reverend Dr. Joe L. Stevenson, Senior Pastor.

Highlights of Reverend Murphy's ministerial service include: mobilizing churches in creating a culture of Evangelism, organizing training sessions, and symposiums for equipping Disciples of Jesus Christ to be effective witnesses, dispersing Christian resources and materials globally from the United States to Africa, Asia, Middle Eastern Nations, and The West Indies and The Caribbean. In addition, Reverend Murphy's works include support to families and communities in the region suffering from the devastating effects of Category Five Hurricanes: working with them during their emergent phase of loss and their restorative phase of re-structuring. During the COVID-19 pandemic in 2020, Reverend Murphy implemented food distribution procedures that served over 12,000 pounds of food to families and communities in Raleigh, North Carolina. Within the first six months of implementation. Reverend Murphy's loving care of God's people and her mantra of giving has inspired and continues to inspire her to provide the vital necessities of living, such as coats, clothing, toiletries, money, and shelter to residents in the local communities.

She enjoys writing and has authored the first edition of her book, *Dissecting L.O.V.E.*, housed in the Library of Congress, in Washington, D.C. In addition, she has also written poetry for *The Carolinian,* the largest African American Newspaper in North Carolina.

Reverend Murphy graduated from Caldwell Community College in 1994, graduated from UNC Greensboro in 2005, and graduated from Apex School of Theology in 2019. She has earned a Registered Nurse License, a Baccalaureate Degree in Nursing, and a Master of Divinity Degree.

She is abundantly blessed in marriage as wife to Mr. William Murphy of 9 years; abundantly blessed as mother to three adult children: Andrea, Devante, Montanna; and abundantly blessed as grandmother to her two grandchildren, London and Amina. They all are a part of her greatest joys and accomplishments in life.

Reverend Murphy's life motto is- "Do all that you can do, and when it seems like you are done, do some more." She has two favorite Scripture references: The Lord's Prayer found in the Gospel of Matthew 6:9-13 and the Words of Jesus Christ found in Saint John 19:30: *"it is finished."*

The Product, The Pieces, and The Platform
(The Power of God's Protection)

"Where unto I am appointed a preacher, and an apostle, and a teacher of the Gentiles. For the which cause I also suffer these: nevertheless, I am not ashamed: for I know whom I have believed and am persuaded that he is able to keep that which I have committed unto him against that day."
2 Timothy 1: 11-12

First, giving honor to my Lord and Savior Jesus Christ. God has been protecting my Christian heritage, my genealogy, and me away from Satan's attempts to destroy them all since my birth. This chapter will speak to the paternal grandparents, the maternal grandparents, and the parents of children who are born with a heritage and heavy calling to preach the Word of God. This chapter aims to gain the attention of these adults so they can resist the notion and urge o keeping the children away from the church. For these are the children who are charged *necessarily* to propel the church onward until the day of the return of our Lord Jesus. This chapter is also written to encourage ministers of the Gospel to continue their forward movement in God's call to serve in ministry solely because of the keeping power of God's protection. God will always protect the product of His Holy Word that lives within us.

When I was born at Mission Hospital in Asheville, North Carolina, it was because my mother was sent there to give birth to me. It was a girls' school and at that time, the young mothers were sent away to training school, especially those who were about to be teen mothers. I was told that upon my birth I was supposed to have been given up for adoption to a white family. There were several reasons for adoption: a) because of my near-white complexion at birth, b) because my mother was a teenager, and c) because my grandmother and great-grandmother were boot-leggers in a nearby mountain city about two hours away. The social worker who lived in the community was familiar with the lifestyles of my grand-mother and great-grandmother. The social worker was a black prominent leader in the community who was a major contributor to the Historical African Methodist Episcopal (AME) Church in the mountain community. From the stories that I've been told by my aunt about my early beginnings in this world, my grandmother and great-grandmother fought for me to remain in our family and against adoption; they fought harder than they had ever fought for anything in their lives! Culturally speaking, there have been many days that I have pondered about how close I came to losing both my black heritage and my Christian heritage as a woman.

My grandmother and great-grandmother were well loved in the community by people inside and outside of the Church and I am certain that the community ties which they had enabled them to be successful in bringing their first grandchild back home to the family. I was baptized at five days old and was brought home. It was no secret that my grandmother, especially, had a tremendous amount of disdain for the social worker who had fought hard to take me away from them. I've often wondered how that made my grandmother feel and if that was one of the most hurtful views of Christians that she had ever encountered, that a woman of the Church, especially a black woman, warring against her. My grandmother always had choice words to say about the social worker, and I don't recall my grandmother going to church like I recall my great grandmother going; perhaps that may have been one reason why.

When I reflect on my early life in this world, I see God's protection from my birth in preparation for the preacher that I was to become. How in the world would God allow this black woman preacher to nearly miss the black experience and the black culture and most especially, the black woman experience by being adopted away from a life where she would see it all live and in color? God nestled me right there in the home with the family that I was born to and destined to be with. God's early protection of His Holy Word within me, started at my birth.

Alcoholism is one disease that I saw very early on in life. By God's Grace, I have never developed a taste or a longing for alcohol, especially liquor, even though I was around alcohol every single day of my life from my newborn days to the age of 21 years old. Yet I have never taken a drink to this day. I've often wondered how God never allowed me to develop a taste for alcohol. I can only attribute it to God's divine protection of the product of His Holy Word within the preacher who was to come. I also attribute not drinking alcohol to seeing the effects of alcoholism on the human body of those who came to our home daily. From being raised in the home of women bootleggers, I saw people have seizures after becoming severely intoxicated. As an eight-year-old, I was grabbing spoons rapidly, as instructed, so that the adults could place the spoons in the mouths of those who were near death from a seizure. "Grab the spoon," they would tell me because as it was commonly believed, the person was in danger of "swallowing their tongue". This was a mistruth that I later learned in nursing school was an impossible occurrence, but, to a child, hearing that was scary enough to convince me to never ever take a drink of that stuff.

The irony of my childhood, my genealogy, and my Christian heritage is that my father was from a very prominent family in the community. The entire paternal side of my family were all prominent members of the same Historical AME Church in the community that the social worker was a member of. In other words, my paternal family was avid churchgoers, and my paternal grandmother was the pianist/organist for the church, a fact which I learned later, as an adult. Such interesting dynamics from my early beginnings included my father, who in addition to being from one of the most prominent families in the community, was an alcoholic. He would attempt to come see me at our home; however, my grandmothers only allowed him to enter to purchase the drinks, not to see me or talk to me. I was told to "go get in the closet" every time he would come by. There is no animosity within me from my grandmothers' choices. Back then, I trusted them immensely to protect me from whatever I was supposed to be protected from. At times, when I got off the school bus, I could witness my father from afar. I realized that my father had a big personality, and he had a reputation in the community of being a street scholar. He was fun-loving and this made him likeable to others. My brother was with me when I would get off the school bus and always hurried me along so that my grandmother's instructions were always followed about not speaking to my father. Yet I could hear my dad yelling out very loudly from that street corner to so many people: "HEY everybody, there goes my daughter. That's my daughter right there!" Admittedly, when I heard those words, I felt a sense of belonging, even though I wasn't allowed around him. My father's side of the family never came to get me or take me to church; after all, what would that have looked like churchgoers and boot-leggers? I only met my paternal grandmother, the church organist/pianist, twice in my life, and that was when someone had died who was acquainted with both sides of the family. I remember her smiling at me, but I do not at all recall it as being loving or genuine. In all honesty, my grandmother and great-grandmother wouldn't have let me go with them or get to know them anyway. What were they protecting me from? Were they protecting me from hypocrisy, were they protecting me from being judged, were they protecting me from being taken away from them? What were they afraid of or could it have just been God's way of protecting the product of His Holy Word in the preacher that was to come?

Like I've said, my grandmother and great-grandmother (mother and daughter) knew everybody in the community, and I mean everybody. There were churchgoers and non-churchgoers alike who came by to purchase liquor. My grandmothers were respected mostly because of their ability to not judge anyone who came by. All people were welcome. They allowed the people to talk freely, listened to their stories and challenges, advised them on various matters, fed them, socialized with them, and gave them odd jobs to do for pay. It was a place where people could hang out all day if they wanted to. The people loved and admired them for their care and concern, non-judgment, and the honor that they bestowed to each and every individual who came across their path. They were strong women and the one thing they did not tolerate was disrespect in their home. The people were allowed to drink, but if anyone tried to get rowdy, my grandmother and great-grandmother handled it very firmly and quickly.

My brother and I spent a lot of time in our room, watching TV, and I read a lot; most of all, I enjoyed coming home from school and getting straight to my homework. Learning was one of the things that I did best. These were my escapes. In my elementary years, my great-grandmother would take me to church camp meetings. I have a vivid memory to this day of one particular time when she took me to church. The service was a long service that went late into the night. My great-grandmother sat in the front row, and I remember her telling me to lie down on the front row because she could see I was sleepy, and the church service was still in session. The people seemed really happy that night about something. I remember my great-grandmother standing there and clapping her hands so joyously. It was dark outside, and we were still at church. She seemed so happy. Little did I know, at the time, that it would be the last time I would ever see my great-grandmother at that little church.

I never saw her enter a church ever again after that night. Never. I remember that my great-grandmother would send food to the camp meetings, but she wouldn't attend. I was too young to know to ask why. Today I would ask her if she had experienced church hurt. I would ask her if she had wanted to do more or was God was calling her to do more. I would ask her if she had been restrained and marginalized from doing so because she was a woman. If my great-grandmother was alive today, I would ask her if she had *informally* or *quietly* held the office of Deacon or Minister. Where did I get this genealogy from? I would ask her if she was not allowed to be what she appeared to be that last night at the church. If so, why? All these things I would ask her now because she really enjoyed the service that night for whatever the reason.

After that experience, some months later, one evening at our home, I opened the door to our room and my great-grandmother was down on her knees, praying. I had never seen that before, so I closed the door very quickly, thinking it was something that I wasn't supposed to see. I remember that my great-grandmother made sure that my brother and I learned and recited the Lord's Prayer every single night.

My other early childhood church experiences were few. What I do remember is that a friend of the family, who was a member of another Methodist church, talked with my grandmother and must have been very persuasive. She convinced my grandmother to allow me to be in the children's choir. This friend of the family was the Children's Choir Director, at a different Methodist church, and since neither my grandmother nor my great-grandmother drove a car, the friend said she would pick me up every Tuesday evening. I am sure that my grandmother agreed because she trusted her. My great-grandmother just always seemed to have a keen sense about knowing when someone was being phony. She knew this was not a phony request from Mrs. M. They truly believed that Mrs. M. really wanted to help me know about church. At the choir practice, I didn't really care for the singing parts; what I really enjoyed was being able to go somewhere besides school and back home. I knew that on Tuesdays, Mrs. M. was going to pick me up and I would get to see the church. The church was so nice, so quiet, so beautiful. You see, as I've reflected over my life, I wasn't even supposed to get to know church, and especially not supposed to learn anything from the Historical AME Church in town. Remember the Historical AME Church was where my paternal family went.

My other great experience as a child was also at church; I'll call it Grace Church. The Grace Church accepted everybody: the non-prominent and the prominent. Everybody was welcome at the Grace Church, the recovering alcoholics, too. The church sat on a hill near our house. From our house, you could hear the music and the foot-stomping on the wooden floors. The Grace Church was unapologetically loud! The people who went there just couldn't help it. What I now know as the Holy Ghost was happening at Grace Church. Each Easter Sunday, my brother and I were told to go to Grace Church. My aunt would take us there most times, but I do remember times when my grandmother and great-grandmother would let us go on our own because they truly honored and trusted the woman who founded Grace Church. My great-grandmother no longer went to church, since that night from the camp meeting, but they both sent us on Easter Sunday. Let us never discredit the power of people's Easter commitment to go to church: there just may be a future little girl preacher in the crowd, learning little bits and pieces about church and unknowingly falling in love with the church.

My most vivid memory of the Grace Church from the ages of 9-12 was the gold-plated offering plate. It was so shiny, and at the time in the service, when the preacher said for everyone to walk up and give, my brother and I had been given coins to place into the offering plate from our grandparents. I just loved to see and hear the coins as they made their way into the offering plate. To me, there was something special about that part of the service, yet I didn't learn about it formally until my late 20s or early 30s. Even then, God was protecting me to make sure that I saw just enough of my Church Heritage. The Pastor of the Grace Church did a lot for the people in the community who people looked past or down upon.

My grandmother and great-grandmother died in 1995 and 1996 respectively. You could say that my brother and I were over-protected; however, we had just enough of God's Divine Protection and just enough church engrained in us to be able to recall when it was truly needed many years later.

After I became Saved, I once asked a Christian friend of mine, introspectively, "I wonder why my grandmother and my great-grandmother never told me about Jesus. Jesus is so *Good*." The answer was, "Yolande, you were in the right place, and they gave you as much as they knew to give you of Christianity." By this, he meant: the Lord's Prayer, being able to see the inside of the Church and the Joy, the service of providing food, the Giving in the Gold Plate, the care of people, and the choir singing. So, I ran with what my friend said, and as an adult, I decided I was determined to know and be connected to Christianity forever. After all, God had protected His product, His vessel, and His Word within me.

My grandmother's name was Glendaile Corpening and her mother, my great-grandmother's, name was Georgia Bridges. They committed me unto the Lord in Baptism at five days old at the Mission Hospital. Could they have even known the seriousness of it all, that they were committing a preacher unto the Lord? I think they did, in some way. They committed me unto the Lord, God's Word is true: *that he is able to keep that which I have committed unto him against that day."* 2 Timothy 1: 11-12

As an adult, after my Confession of Salvation and after the acceptance of my calling in ministry as a Woman of God, Satan's attempts to destroy my Christian Heritage, my Genealogy, and me did not stop even while I was serving in ministry. In other words, there were satanic attacks that tried to rip me to *Pieces:* emotionally, psychologically, physically, and spiritually. These attacks ranged in variety and presented in the form of many challenges such as fatigue/exhaustion, joblessness, homelessness, family disputes, being penniless, living paycheck to paycheck, physical pain, criminal injustice, racial profiling, rage, depression, sorrow, car wreckage, rejection, grief/loss, fragile family members, feelings of inadequacy, and envy. These poundings and overloads of stressors would sometimes occur simultaneously, repeatedly, and seemingly endlessly to the point of near anguish and lifelessness. The difference from my childhood was that now, I knew how to choose Church! I chose everything about the Church: The Bible Study, the Prayer Meetings, the Word of God, the Servitude, the Worship, the Giving, everything, and more!

My Christian heritage, my genealogy, and I were not up for grabs anymore! There was no one telling me to go get in the closet away from my Heavenly Father! There was no one telling me not to know my Father in Heaven and His Glorious Son, Jesus Christ! Being fully aware of my rights and responsibilities as a Christian kept me fully persuaded. I knew that every satanic attack that the devil tried to throw in my direction to try to keep me away from my heritage in Christ Jesus was only temporary. Almighty God was holding the pieces of every part of my life together, which enabled me to grasp Christianity and to hold on tight to Christianity and to propel to the Platform which enables me to triumphantly proclaim and declare the Gospel Good News!

"Where unto I am appointed a preacher, and an apostle, and a teacher of the Gentiles. For the which cause I also suffer these: nevertheless, I am not ashamed: for I know whom I have believed and am persuaded that he is able to keep that which I have committed unto him against that day."
2 Timothy 1: 11-12

This chapter is dedicated to my Spiritual Father in Ministry: Bishop Rev. Dr. Joe. L. Stevenson, Senior Pastor of Macedonia New Life Church, Raleigh, North Carolina who has never instructed me to hide away in a closet but has strongly encouraged my life in the knowledge of Jesus Christ, my belonging in the Family of God, and my Full Proclamation of God's Holy Word as a Woman of God in Ministry.

Chapter 11

Dr. Monica D. Redmond

Dr. Monica D. Redmond

Reverend Dr. Monica D. Redmond is a native of Columbia, South Carolina, the second of five children born to the late Rev. Grant E. Redmond and Rev. Clorine Redmond. She is uniquely gifted and is heralded as one of the Body of Christ's most prolific and insightful speakers. Drawing from her own personal experiences, Dr. Redmond is especially anointed to minister a word of spiritual healing and wholeness.

It was while a student at Winthrop University in Rock Hill, South Carolina that she was called to preach. After much prayer and fasting, Dr. Redmond preached her initial sermon on July 10, 1988. She subsequently received a Bachelor of Science Degree in Business and Finance from Winthrop in May 1989. On June 26, 1994, the Mount Peace Missionary Baptist Association set Dr. Redmond apart and ordained her for the work of the gospel ministry. Sensing the need for further education and preparation, Dr. Redmond pursued theological and ministerial training at Hood Theological Seminary in Salisbury, North Carolina, and is a 1996 Master of Divinity cum laude graduate. Her terminal degree is the Doctor of Ministry degree which was conferred upon her by the Morehouse School of Religion at the Interdenominational Theological Center in Atlanta, Georgia. Her doctoral dissertation is entitled, "Finding A Missional Church Identity." Reverend Dr. Redmond is a cum laude graduate and was recognized for her scholarly work and inducted into the International Society of Theta Phi, an honor society for theological students and scholars in the field of religion and outstanding religious leaders.

In addition to her passionate pursuit of education, Reverend Dr. Redmond is a faithful member of St. Paul Baptist Church in Charlotte, North Carolina. Reverend Dr. Robert C. Scott is the Senior Pastor and Reverend Dr. Redmond serves as the Executive Pastor. St. Paul's missiological thrust is to "convince the unconvinced to be convinced and make disciples." Reverend Dr. Redmond's focus on building a person holistically echoes this mission.

Her personal philosophy is, "*As far as I am concerned, to live is Christ but to die is gain. Therefore, I am living now as one whose life is hidden in Christ so that one day, I, too, might live with Him. If I can help somebody along the way, then my living is not in vain.*"

I'm Preaching with a Limp

Early Beginnings

As I sit here today and reflect on a 36-year preaching career, I can't help but think about where it all began. I was born on January 1, 1966, the second of five children born to Grant and Clorine Redmond. As my parents told me every January 1, I was supposed to be a boy! Their intention when they married was to have only two children, a boy, and a girl. My sister Angela was their firstborn and when Mom was pregnant with me, she naturally assumed that I would be a boy and she and Dad would have the total package they had hoped and prayed for. They even had a name already picked out for their secondborn, Monty Dupree Redmond. Well, as fate would have it, their secondborn wasn't a boy, but a girl! On January 1, 1966, at approximately 4:00 am, Monica Denise Redmond burst on the scene! I came with a lot of fanfare too, not because I was born specifically but because it was the new year! It took me a while to learn that the fireworks going off every January 1st had nothing to do with me, but I sincerely believed that it did. Mom and Dad were happy about their surprise, but Dad still wanted a boy! They kept trying, ending up with four girls before they got their boy!

I loved my early childhood growing up at the corner of Route 2, Telfair Street and Hollywood Lane in Fountain Inn, South Carolina. For those of you wondering where Fountain Inn is located, it is about 17 miles to the northwest of Greenville, South Carolina, and 84 miles to the southeast of Columbia, South Carolina. I loved its simplicity, with red dirt roads and green plush grass and woods for my sister and me to play Goldie Locks and the Three Bears. It was an exciting place to allow our childhood imaginations to run wild!

Another reason why I loved living in Fountain Inn is it allowed us to be near both mom and dad's families. Mom was the fourth child of eleven and Daddy was the fourth child of five children, and they lived in Fountain Inn. Living there allowed us to remain close to my aunts, uncles, and cousins who lived in Greenville, South Carolina and the surrounding cities and towns, making it possible for us to visit them often.

My grandfather was a preacher and mom's family had a lot of celebrity in the area because the entire family could sing. Every year at Thanksgiving, the Sherman Family would host the Sherman Family Anniversary where they would sing and testify to the goodness of the Lord! I loved it because gospel choirs and quartet groups from all over North and South Carolina would gather at my grandfather's church. Our family motto was, "A family that prays together stays together!"

I didn't know of anything else but the church in those first years of my life. My dad started preaching and pastoring the year I was born. My grandfather preached and founded two churches, several of my uncles preached, and eventually, several of my cousins preached as well. So church is all I knew!

When I was seven, Dad moved us from Fountain Inn to Columbia, South Carolina because of a new job opportunity. I distinctly remember those years because my spiritual formation was deepening. I didn't realize it at the time, but I was an inquisitive child. So inquisitive that I read every book I could get my hands on. Some of you may or may not remember the Weekly Reader as I do, but the Weekly Reader fortified my childhood curiosity. I couldn't help it; I read everything I could put my hands on! It drove my parents crazy at times, only because I'd rather read a book than go outside and play.

I remember reading about Curious George and Amelia Bedelia. "I also remember reading about Ramona and Beezus! But the book that changed my life as a young girl was when I read, *Are You Their God? It's Me, Margaret.*" This book is about an eleven-year-old girl who moves to a new town, and she begins contemplating everything about life, friendship, and adolescence. Her story became my story as it spoke to my own curiosity about my identity and my place in this world. I was fascinated as I read this book because little eleven-year-old Margaret begins to talk to God. She talked to Him about menial topics such as being able to belong, how she wants to grow, and how she wants Him to be proud of her. She talked to Him about being afraid, about having a new friend and wanting to mature physically. She talked to God so easily that I began to thirst to talk to Him as well.

This book drove me to talk to my parents about God and getting baptized and what that meant. So, after talking with my parents, this young girl, at 10 years old, made a decision for Jesus Christ and was baptized by her father, becoming a member of the New Hope Baptist Church in Columbia, South Carolina. My Dad served this church as the pastor and my mom was the first lady! What is interesting about my newfound relationship with God is my thirst and hunger to know more about Him. I wanted to please God in the same way that Margaret wanted to please Him.

So, I went to Sunday School and Bible study, and I got on my knees every night by my bed, and I would talk to God just like Margaret did! My sisters and I sang in the youth choir and eventually we formed a singing group and named it after our father, the Reverend Grant Edward Redmond. We officially became the G.E. Redmond Singers. We started singing not only at New Hope Baptist Church, but we would sing at surrounding churches in Columbia as well!

To be honest, in those early years, I really was unbelievably shy and preferred to remain in the background. So much so that people would ask, "Where's Monica?" and I would be sitting in the same room. But you know what? My elementary, middle school, and high school teachers saw something different in me. I credit them all with pulling me from the background to the front! This period in my life was during the time when teachers would ask you to read out loud in class. As a matter of fact, because of that, one teacher encouraged me to join the drama club. When I did, somehow, I always had the leading role. One year we performed *God's Trombones: Seven Negro Sermons in Verse,* by James Weldon Johnson. That opportunity changed my life!

When I became a senior my teachers, my early mentors, again pushed me to become the class speaker. "Who, me, I asked?" They responded and said, "Yes, you." My classmates agreed. At graduation, in 1984, I was the graduation speaker for the Columbia High School graduating class. I remember starting my speech by saying, "Success is not reached in a single bound. We mount to its summit round by round!" I really didn't know what I was saying back then, but my favorite teacher and mentor, Mrs. Pauline Davis, told me those words would be a great way to open my speech. I understand those words now because success for me is still being realized, round by round as I keep on mounting!

My Undergraduate College Years

Eventually, after graduating from Columbia High School in 1984, I left Columbia and moved to Rock Hill, South Carolina to pursue a bachelor's degree in business and finance. At Winthrop College, Business and Finance wasn't what I wanted to major in, but I did it because an adult in my life told me if I majored in social work, which matched my heart's desire to help people, that I wouldn't make any money. I don't think I did very well, but I graduated! That experience taught me to follow my dreams and I encouraged young people from that point on to follow their passions.

In 1988, while still a student at Winthrop College, this shy young girl was called to preach. It shocked a lot of people, including my parents, but I know I heard the voice of God, one night in what I thought were my dreams, commanding me to "Go ye therefore and preach my Gospel!" So, on July 10, 1988, I preached my initial sermon entitled, "A Brand-New Me," using 2 Corinthians 5:17 as my sermonic scripture. I didn't go back home after graduation because a friend of mine told me about a Church in Charlotte, North Carolina that I needed to consider! He knew I wanted to belong to a church that recognized and affirmed women preachers, so he said to me that I should at least consider it.

After College

So, I checked this church out and I joined it after visiting four consecutive Sundays. What impressed me so much about this church was not only the good preaching and teaching from the Senior Pastor and glorious singing from the choirs on Sunday mornings but what caught my eye the most were the women in the pulpit! These women weren't just sitting in the pulpit, but they were serving by reading scripture, praying, and even preaching at times! After much prayer and fasting this church became my home!

This pastor was key in my spiritual and ministerial development. After allowing me to preach for the first time at New Year's Eve Watch Night Service, this pastor encouraged me to go to seminary to continue developing the gift of preaching he saw in me. I listened to him, and in August of 1993, I enrolled at Hood Theological Seminary in Salisbury, North Carolina, eventually graduating with honors in 1996. I was excited about this church and the opportunities that this church afforded me. But it was here also where I began to see my *preaching gift* as a limp. Yes, for the first time, I felt that preaching and being a female had its limitations. My father, grandfather, and new pastor embraced my gift, but throughout North and South Carolina, the feeling was not the same!

For instance, in 1994, when I, along with three other women, were presented for ordination, we were confronted with gender bias head-on. Even though the moderator said the association was delighted for the first time to ordain women, the certificates we received did not reveal that same elation. Looking back, it was blatant gender bias when we saw the word *him* in the sentence with a black x across it and the word *her* written just above it! Would it have hurt to just have certificates with her in the sentence? Well, this was a first for me, but it certainly was not the last. From being invited to preach to being told I would have to preach on the floor instead of the pulpit after I arrived. But, through it all, I didn't argue, and I couldn't be dissuaded, so I continued to preach the gospel!

Seminary Years (First Limp)

While in Seminary, I was moved by an article that was written by Karen Garloch, staff writer for the Charlotte Observer, which read:

When she was five or six, Winifred Kollie was taken to the "Sande Bush," a secret society where girls in her rural Liberian tribe learned how to cook and weave baskets and be good wives.

It is also where she was circumcised. Using a razor and no anesthetic, an elderly woman, a leader of the tribe, removed Kollie's clitoris in a revered ritual that her mother and grandmother proudly expected her to carry on.

Through the eyes of a young woman brought up in Western culture my initial reaction to that practice was shock. I wondered, how could a people be so callous and brutal with no regard for human life? The World Health Organization regarded the ritual as demoralizing and degrading so much so that they blatantly condemned the act. But you know what? As I continued to read this article, I could not ignore the possibility of my own naiveté, therefore, I committed myself to exploring the alternatives. I began asking questions of the writing such as, is this practice genital mutilation, as our culture perceives it, or is it the rural African equivalent of religion?

From a culturally biased perception, this was a bizarre, heinous crime. From a missiological standpoint, however, that was a tradition that expressed a strongly felt need within the community. In other words, the ritual was part of what that culture perceived to be religion. It was another culture, unlike my own, seeking to carry out the practices of its society.

Church History, Christian Missions, and Missiology which I revered while in seminary have all shown that Western culture has sought to assume the role as a pacesetter toward the perfect culture. But is this culture perfect? Of course not! Don't you know that even in that same seminary where I wrestled with these questions about cultural bias, I was confronted with gender bias right there!

In my homiletics class, for instance, after I preached my first sermon before the class, the professor, instead of giving me constructive criticism, used the moment to be sexist and demoralizing. I refuse to repeat his remarks because I don't want to memorialize bigotry! For forty-five minutes he disrobed and insulted me! I felt dehumanized because of that experience. But you know what I learned? I learned that I'm not responsible for what people say to discredit me, but I am responsible for how I respond.

So, I responded by continuing to go to class. I continued to preach and learn, and the next time I preached in class he could only say, Ms. Redmond, you are anointed! From that experience what I learned to do is just keep on preaching the gospel because God will ultimately change the hearts and minds of the listener. My job is to fulfill what I've been called to do and that is to preach!

My Medical Diagnosis (Second Limp)

Allow me to digress for a moment to a time when I served as a youth minister at a large Baptist Church in Charlotte, North Carolina. While there, going to camp with the kids, counseling them, and being their friend, a nagging feeling reappeared. There was burning and tingling in my hands and feet. This burning and tingling feeling, which I had felt for many years, was back with a vengeance. It was becoming worse and worse. I knew something was wrong with me, but my doctors couldn't diagnose the problem. They said everything from lupus to depression. For as long as I could remember, the tingling and numbness would come, and it would go.

It persisted through undergraduate school and even in seminary. But in 1997, the problem seemed to be progressing because, in addition to the burning and tingling under my skin, my right foot began to drag, and I was numb on the entire right side of my body. I knew I needed some answers, so I made an appointment to see a new doctor. This doctor examined me and recommended that I see a neurologist. I went to see this neurologist and he examined me and ordered an MRI. I felt some relief because this doctor seemed vigilant about finding out what was wrong with me. I was to have the MRI on Wednesday and my neurologist told me that if he hadn't called me by that Friday, then everything was fine, and he would keep searching for an answer to my problem. Friday came and went and there was no call from my doctor. I went the entire weekend and there was no call. Then, Monday came. I thought everything was fine until I called home and checked my voicemail messages. The doctor had left a message saying that my tests had come back abnormal and that I needed to contact him right away. When I did, he suggested that I come in to see him. Naturally, I was a nervous wreck before that appointment. All kinds of thoughts went through my mind. Was it a brain tumor? Was I dying? I didn't know.

I will never forget the day I went into his office to receive the diagnosis. I went alone that day because I had calmed down and convinced myself that everything was going to be all right. But God only knows how I made it through those brief moments that seemed like a lifetime. The doctor came in and said to me, Ms. Redmond your tests reveal what looks like Multiple Sclerosis. Immediately my thoughts began to spin out of control. Multiple Sclerosis? What's that? I'd heard it before, but I couldn't remember where I had heard it. And then my mind began to register the faces of Richard Pryor, Annette Funnicello, and Lola Falana. And then, I *really* lost it. This doctor must be mistaken because Richard Pryor can't walk. Annette Funnicello is in a wheelchair. And I couldn't think of where Lola Falana had been. He must be talking to the wrong person. I had just finished seminary and I was working at my dream job! He must mean someone else. But he wasn't mistaken. By the end of the hour, I was totally out of control. I was unreasonable and he had to call his nurse into the room to calm me down. Yes, this preaching girl was losing it. However, the nurse was able to calm me down long enough for the doctor to discuss the different medications that were available. I couldn't believe it because now I had another limp! Who wants to hire a sick preacher I asked myself? Should I quit because I didn't think I could continue to preach with this limp?

The neurologist then offered that there were medications approved by the FDA that he suggested I should start taking immediately. Of course, I refused and took the denial route. That was my Plan A: ignore this disease and it will just go away. "Pretend that it is not there" became my mantra. It sounded like a pretty good plan back then.

What's so unfortunate about this plan is that it was reinforced by the church I called home. My church told me not to claim it, so I didn't. My church suggested that I not take the medication and I didn't. My church taught me that if you just have faith and sincerely claimed God's promises, then you don't need the medication because belief and trust in God was all I needed.

Well, the plan of denying this disease and refusing the medication was not working for me because the longer I pretended that it wasn't there the worse I became. That, of course, was the early days of my disease. Today, after much prayer along with chemotherapy, steroids, Tysabri infusions, and the other drugs that have been approved by the FDA, you can't look at me and see multiple sclerosis. If it had not been for the wise statements of a mentor who walked alongside me through this journey, I don't believe that I would have progressed so favorably. She made one statement that changed my thinking. She said, "Monica, God will use whatever method He needs to use to bring about your healing." "Have faith," she said, "that God has directed your doctor to the right medication to bring about your healing." My friend and mentor walked alongside me in those early days of this very cruel disease and I'm better because of her wisdom!

I close by saying, *mentors matter*! In every aspect of my life, having a mentor has made all the difference! For each woman reading this book, allow me to offer some advice for the road:

1. God called you to preach, so allow Him to send you!
2. Your gift will make room for you.
3. Continue to develop and grow as a preacher.
4. Go where God leads.
5. Since you have the call, listen!

SALUTING BLACK WOMEN PREACHERS
WHO LIVED THE CALL

The biographical sketches are quoted directly from Candice Benbow's article, "Black women preachers who changed-and are changing-history" (Benbow, 2022). They each reflect historical witness of the resilience and current expression of a courage that must be fueled by the Holy Sprit's power and presence.

> *The Rev. Wil Gafney, Ph.D. - Gafney is an Episcopal priest, former army chaplain and congregational pastor in the AME Zion Church. A professor of Hebrew Bible, Gafney's searing biblical analysis grounds her works "Womanist Midrash: A Reintroduction to Women of the Torah and of the Throne and Daughters of Miriam: Women Prophets in Ancient Israel." She is also co-editor of "The Peoples' Bible and The Peoples' Companion to the Bible." Gafney's latest work, "A Women's Lectionary for the Whole Church," builds an entire lectionary centering the stories, voices and experiences of women—and Black women, in particular.*

> *Bishop Yvette A. Flunder - Flunder is the Founder and Senior Pastor of City of Refuge United Church of Christ in Oakland, California. She is also the Presiding Bishop of The Fellowship of Affirming Ministries, which is grounded in a theology of radical inclusivity. Considered a beloved pastor of the movement, Bishop Flunder identifies her call as to "blend proclamation, worship, service and advocacy on behalf of those most marginalized in church and in society." An award-winning gospel artist, Flunder is also the author of "Where the Edge Gathers: Building a Community of Radical Inclusion."*

Chapter 12

Rev. Toshiba Rice

Rev. Toshiba Rice

Toshiba Rice, known as "T. Rice," is a multifaceted individual whose career spans entrepreneurship, community leadership, and spiritual guidance. With over 25 years of experience, she has been a trusted consultant tackling complex issues within local communities, in North Carolina. T. Rice has held numerous citizen leadership positions, contributing her expertise to various committees and boards such as the Chair of the City of Raleigh's Forestville Rd. Citizens Advisory Council and member of Wake County Human Services Northern Regional Center Citizen Advisory Council. She is actively involved in civic organizations like the Education Committee of the Raleigh/Wake-Apex NAACP. Currently, T. Rice serves as the Secretary of Raleigh Interdenominational Ministerial Alliance, the C.E.O and Principal Well-being Consultant at imWell, the Pastor of Greater Faith Raleigh, and a proud Wake County Public School System board member representing District 4 and the largest school district in North Carolina.

Toshiba is a sought-after, confident national speaker and trainer, empowering all to live well and focus on self-care. She has embraced the task of change without masking pain behind a smile. The ability to be open and transparent is her monogram character to express her freedom in Christ. Toshiba is an honored mother to four sons, Joshua, Khyari (deceased), Kimani, and Nicholas. Grandmother to two granddaughters, Layla and Makenzie who call her "MiMi". Toshiba lives to be H.A.P.P.Y. and clothe in G.R.A.C.E. Her signature statement to all, *Have a positive and productive day!*[SM]

Handpicked for the Harvest

"Before I formed you in the womb I knew you, and before you were born, I consecrated you; I appointed you a prophet to the nations."
(Jeremiah 1:5 ESV)

I Know You

Legs straddled and confused at Duke Hospital in Durham, North Carolina, by the hands she sees in labor and delivery. A seventeen-year-old single mother, with no parents, both dead by the time she was eight, lay puzzled while in pain. "Those hands are too big.", her mind wonders in thought, pushing once more. The baby girl is released and falls into those big hands. This is the story my prophetic mother recalls about my birth. Years later, the girl, now a woman and prophetess, realizes they were the hands of God.

This story always amazes me because my earliest memory of an encounter with God was at five years old. I was sitting on my aunt's front steps, in Franklinton, North Carolina, one Sunday afternoon, as I sang my heart to a song that was playing on the record player. Tears rolled down my face. I saw a bubble luring down from heaven towards me, as I sat and sang. When it got closer and turned towards me. It was the face of Jesus that I could identify as a child. I was so shocked and afraid. I ran into the house to my mother and told her what I saw. That day feels like yesterday and serves as a catalyst to encourage others to know God hears us, will meet us at any stage and age of life, and make His presence known. It's by God's grace that my life has triumphed, and God continues to keep showing up in miraculous ways.

By His GRACE, I have seen and accomplished so much. Not material possessions alone, but a quality of life that money can't purchase. This life or lived experiences, gives me peace so deep that if today was my eternal resting day, it would be well with my soul. Some call it, self-actualization. In my consulting firm, I call it wholeheartedly, enjoying living life, when I say, I'm Well!

That's what this journey has been for me. Wholeheartedly, enjoying living life while actively participating in the grace of God delivering me from guilt and shame. I, too, was a single mother of three sons at age twenty-two. Two are twins. This single mother's journey had challenges with many obstacles along the way, particularly from the faith community I loved so much. The anointing of God and being chosen by God has a way to allow his grace to triumph. Not only for the choices I made but just because I was picked for the harvest. Here is the obstacle and triumphant timeline from seed to harvest.

The Seed

In 1982, at age 8, I was baptized by water. I attended fellowship for one dollar. I would receive fifty cents, as promised by my friend if I attended. Upon arrival, I was greeted with a harvest of youth. I fell in love with everyone. As I embraced these new faces that became familiar, I was not always treated with open arms. I loved God, at such a young age, and knew he was good. These weekly trips were not accompanied by my guardian. I was a youngster on fire for God. Baptized with the Holy Ghost at age 10, I loved and chased after God. My prayer was, *Lord, save my mother and father.* Over time, my mother started to come and fellowship with me and was filled with the Holy Ghost. Things at home began to change but my parents' relationship ended in divorce. My household was turned upside down. Life as I formally knew it was over.

In 1993, I had my first child, at 20 years old. I had three children by the time I was 22. My children's father proposed after our first child. I accepted the proposal with a beautiful pear-shaped diamond ring but later returned it with a desire not to marry him. During that time, I found out that I had gotten pregnant with the twins while we were engaged. My former fiancé turned to me, while we were in the hospital because I had passed out at work and said, "I know you will marry me now since we're gonna have three children." I turned to him and said, "No, I'm not." Many people thought that I was out of my mind! I was told that it was better that I marry and worry about potential divorce later, than not marry him at all. A young woman with three children and not wanting to marry the father went against every principle and everything that I knew.

The Cultivation

Focused on God with everything in me, I taught my children how to pray and call on the name of the Lord. I changed my entire behavior to raise my sons to fear, love, and trust God under any circumstances. I believed that God had something better for me. I believed that, although I made unwise choices, God understood and knew my choice, in the end, would work out for my good. I suffered ridicule, was an outcast, and felt like I was not a child of God. At some point, I believed that even though I was repairing my intimate relationship with Christ, I still believed that I was going to hell. I believed because I had sex and children out of wedlock, there was no other option but hell. It was ingrained in me that because I made unhealthy choices out of hurt, pain, and misunderstanding that I was doing to hell.

I love God so greatly; I was willing to do all the things that were right in the eyes of the church that I did not care if I was still going to go to hell, even though I was trying to do everything that the scriptures were telling me to do. I was just excited to be in God's presence and know that I was loved by Him if no one else loved me. It is in these moments that I learned how to love others and how to show others grace no matter what choices they made.

I did not do everything right, but it is understanding grace that changed my life. Test and trials of watching others not handle things with grace taught me how to handle people with long spoons of forgiveness. Allowing others to be their genuine selves, free, to witness their self-discovery of Christ. Exploring the knowing of who the son sets free is free indeed. Giving them the grace to wholeheartedly enjoy life. This process did not come overnight, but it came with time and living through life's highs and lows. I survived a marriage that ended after 18 years while living with a spouse with severe mental illness, children with mental and chronic illnesses, and 10 deaths that included my twin son, close family member, and childhood friends, all within 15 months. I want to share how life changed for me when I applied grace.

The Harvest

The once single mother who no one thought would ever be anything and wasn't good enough allowed God to show me his plan for my life. God said I am enough because He is enough. His grace allowed me to return to school, where I received certifications and trainings. I am the CEO and Principal Wellbeing Trainer and Consultant, of my firm, imWell. I train nationally in Mental Health First Aid. I accepted the call to pastor the unchurched, those seeking spiritual direction, and believers who left the organized faith. I became a strong community leader who speaks truth to power concerning complex issues. This grace anointing destroyed barriers to allow me to serve the largest school district in the state of North Carolina and the 15th largest school district in the United States, as the ninth African American on the Wake County Public School Board. The moment that completed the out show of grace was the invitation from my childhood faith community, Suffragan Bishop of the NC Pentecostal Churches of the Apostolic Faith, to come present on mental health. This Healthy Church Summit was the full circle moment for me. All the things I saw, within the faith community, that may have caused harm or misunderstood for a healthy lifestyle were addressed with open hearts to receive more. Learning how to embrace faith, focus on self-care, and address mental health within yourself, those you love, and the church.

The success of being a single mother, divorcee, pastor, school board member, grandmother, and resilient after the death of a child, is not a simple task. It took an action plan to get me there. Psalms 32:8-9 declares, *"I will instruct you and teach you in the way you should go; I will counsel you with my eye upon you."* The LORD says, *"I will guide you along the best pathway for your life. I will advise you and watch over you. Faith without works is dead."* To live well we must execute a plan of action. I call it the G.R.A.C.E action plan.

Clothe in G.R.A.C.E

Genuine Connection:
Foster genuine connections with yourself and others by being open and sincere in your interactions.

My appointment affirming ceremony to the Wake County Public School Board was standing room only. It included the attendance of elected officials from state to local government, clergy community members, school friends, family, community colleagues, and business partners. They were there because they all had a genuine connection with me. Attendance ranged from my oldest friend from second grade to my most recent business relationship over two decades. One state official yelled, "We love you, Toshiba". That room demonstrated genuine connections.

I was able to foster these relationships because I had to be honest with myself. Ask myself what my motive was for connecting with them. Ask how or where I fit in their life's plan. How does God want me to connect with them? When we focus on genuine connection, I often find the person being an answered prayer or I am for them. My connections mean something. Many said, "Toshiba, this room is just a reflection of the love you have given the community." Pure joy comes from seeing love demonstrated with genuine connections. This practice makes it easy to spot someone challenged by false humility. Their actions or intentionality often stand out to me when looking through a spiritual lens. Discernment reveals motives but fruit from their intentions is what exposes the truth. I find being genuine with everyone I connect with makes future interactions easier and engagement honest.

Resilience Building:
Cultivate resilience by facing challenges with strength and flexibility, learning from setbacks, and bouncing back stronger.

I have mastered resilience and teach others. My belief is I will always rise if God is with me. Resilience building is a dynamic process that involves cultivating the ability to face challenges with strength and flexibility. It begins with a mindset that embraces difficulties as opportunities for growth rather than insurmountable obstacles. By maintaining a positive outlook and staying adaptable, individuals can navigate through life's adversities more effectively. This flexibility allows for the exploration of different solutions and strategies, fostering a sense of empowerment and control. When confronted with setbacks, instead of succumbing to defeat, resilient individuals assess the situation, learn from their experiences, and adjust their approach. This proactive attitude not only helps in overcoming immediate challenges but also builds a foundation for handling future obstacles with greater ease.

Learning from setbacks is a crucial component of resilience building. Each failure or disappointment provides valuable lessons that contribute to personal growth and development. By reflecting on what went wrong and identifying areas for improvement, individuals can turn their experiences into steppingstones for success. This process of continuous learning and adaptation strengthens their resolve and equips them with the skills needed to tackle future challenges. As they bounce back from setbacks, they do so with increased confidence and a deeper understanding of their own capabilities. Over time, this cyclical process of facing challenges, learning, and rebounding creates a resilient mindset that not only withstands adversity but thrives in the face of it.

Authenticity Practice:
Embrace authenticity by staying true to your values, beliefs, and feelings, and expressing yourself genuinely in all aspects of life.

Embracing authenticity involves a steadfast commitment to staying true to your values, beliefs, and feelings, and expressing yourself genuinely in all aspects of life. This begins with self-awareness—understanding what you truly stand for and what matters most to you. By identifying and embracing your core values, you create a reliable compass that guides your decisions and actions. Authenticity requires courage to maintain these values, even when faced with societal pressures or expectations that might tempt you to compromise. It's about being honest with yourself and others, ensuring that your outward actions align with your inner principles. This congruence fosters a sense of inner peace and integrity and helps build trust in your relationships, as others can see and feel your sincerity.

Living authentically also means communicating your thoughts and emotions openly and without pretense. It involves expressing your true self in every interaction, without fear of judgment or rejection. When you consistently act in accordance with your beliefs and feelings, you cultivate an environment of transparency and trust. This genuine expression encourages deeper connections and more meaningful relationships, as it allows others to see and appreciate the real you. Practicing authenticity not only enhances your own sense of fulfillment and well-being but also sets a positive example for those around you. By being unapologetically yourself, you inspire others to do the same, creating a culture of mutual respect and genuine connection. Living authentically also means communicating your thoughts and emotions openly and without pretense. It involves expressing your true self in every interaction, without fear of judgment or rejection. When you consistently act in accordance with your beliefs and feelings, you cultivate an environment of transparency and trust. This genuine expression encourages deeper connections and more meaningful relationships, as it allows others to see and appreciate the real you. Practicing authenticity not only enhances your own sense of fulfillment and well-being but also sets a positive example for those around you. By being unapologetically yourself, you inspire others to do the same, creating a culture of mutual respect and genuine connection.

Charismatic Presence:
Develop a charismatic presence by exuding confidence, positivity, and warmth, and inspiring others through your authentic self.

Developing a charismatic presence involves exuding warmth, confidence, confidence, and positivity which collectively inspire and attract others. Confidence is the cornerstone of charisma; it comes from a deep-seated belief in your abilities and a clear understanding of your worth. When you are confident, you project an aura of assurance that others find compelling and trustworthy. This self-assuredness should be balanced with positivity, as an optimistic outlook not only uplifts your own spirits but also creates a welcoming and encouraging environment for those around you. By approaching situations and interactions with a positive mindset, you can foster goodwill and motivate others to see possibilities rather than obstacles.

Warmth is the quality that connects your confidence and positivity to others on a personal level. It involves showing genuine interest in and empathy for those you interact with, making them feel valued and understood. Warmth can be conveyed through open body language, active listening, and sincere communication. This authenticity is crucial; it ensures that your charisma is not perceived as mere performance but as a true reflection of who you are. When you consistently express your authentic self, you build deeper, more meaningful connections. This genuine charisma not only draws people to you but also inspires them to embrace their own authenticity, creating a ripple effect of positive influence and mutual respect.

Evolve Continuously:
Commit to personal growth and development by continuously learning, adapting, and evolving into the best version of yourself.

Committing to personal growth and development involves a continuous process of learning, adapting, and evolving into the best version of yourself. This journey begins with a mindset that values curiosity and embraces change as a vital component of self-improvement. By actively seeking new knowledge and experiences, you expand your understanding and capabilities, allowing you to navigate life's challenges with greater competence and confidence. Continuous learning is not limited to formal education; it includes learning from everyday experiences, seeking feedback, and being open to new perspectives. This relentless pursuit of growth fuels your adaptability, enabling you to adjust to changing circumstances and seize new opportunities.

Evolving continuously also means regularly reflecting on your progress and setting new goals that push you beyond your comfort zone. Personal development is a dynamic process that requires you to reassess and redefine your aspirations as you grow. By embracing challenges and viewing setbacks as learning opportunities, you build resilience and a stronger sense of self. This commitment to evolution cultivates a proactive attitude toward life, where you take charge of your growth rather than passively waiting for change to happen. As you evolve, you not only enhance your own life but also positively impact those around you, inspiring others to pursue their own paths of growth and development.

My charismatic presence is an evolving force, continuously shaped by the trials and triumphs I encounter. It is through this evolution that I am able to inspire and uplift others, demonstrating that resilience is not just about enduring hardships, but about growing stronger and more compassionate because of them. By embracing continuous growth and self-improvement, I strive to be a beacon of hope and a testament to the power of perseverance, showing that even in the face of adversity, one can emerge with greater strength and purpose. It is my hope to celebrate you as you make the choice to be H.A.P.P.Y.[SM] (hooray, a positive productive you) living in G.R.A.C.E.[SM]

Chapter 13

Dr. Shalonda Schoonmaker

Dr. Shalonda Schoonmaker

Dr. Shalonda S. Schoonmaker was born and raised in Detroit, Michigan, and relocated to Atlanta, Georgia, in 2003, being one of the first in her family to leave the nest. She embarked upon a successful career as an Industry Flight Attendant for sixteen years, retiring in 2020. In 2016, she answered the call to serve women and young girls by founding Shiloh Almah Restoration/SAR4Teengirls, which provides support in the areas of Domestic Violence, Suicide Intervention and Prevention, Human Sex-Trafficking, and Anger Management. This opportunity has allowed her to serve over 1000 women and girls.

Dr. Shalonda started the journey of seminary school in 2018 obtaining a Bachelor of Arts in Pastoral Counseling, then a Master of Arts in Life Coaching, and finally, a Doctorate in Christian Counseling. She became a licensed and ordained Minister and Chaplain in 2019 and is now an ordained Co-Pastor of Spirit and Life Outreach Church. Dr. Schoonmaker is currently serving youth in education.

Dr. Shalonda has a unique testimony and story to tell the world from personal experiences, starting from the streets of her hometown of Detroit as a young woman to relocating solely and starting over in an unfamiliar place. Her raw transparency is sure to pique your interest as you journey with her throughout life as a domestic violence survivor, to a traveler of the United States, to becoming a pastor's wife, to an inspiring author, co-pastor, and Life Coach.

You can follow her authorship journey and debut via Facebook at:
Dr. Shalonda Ministries.
You can connect directly with Dr. Shalonda via email or by visiting her websites:
Email: Dr.S@SAR4Teengirls.com
Websites: www.Spiritandlifechurchglobal.com
www.SAR4Teengirls.com

Caged Bird Singing

Many times, in the ladder seasons of my adult life, I found myself in an epiphanic state relevant to current situations or experiences, directly connected to and triggered by my past. As I reflect on the crucial moment in time, late summer of 2018, I was ironically, fully prepared to transition into ministry and Seminary School. The school was offering a Chaplaincy Program that my husband and I mutually agreed to complete together. We were both excited and fired up for Christ through our Courthouse and Street Outreach Ministry. After enrollment, the Lord spoke to my husband, and we joined the ministry attached to the Seminary School. I was delighted once the Lord had spoken due to the longevity of the Church and its well-seasoned, accomplished leaders. Shortly thereafter, leadership approached my husband about pastoring the church as a successor. We were excited to see spoken words over our marriage and lives begin to manifest. I was looking forward to learning all that I could from a powerful couple about organizational leadership, finance, and church structure. I was also yearning to deepen my spiritual journey, gifts, and relationship with Christ. Despite the normal growing pains of inheriting an established ministry, we jumped right into our roles as "Pastor and First Lady" in training. We also experienced our fair share of unreceptiveness from the congregation. We did, however, stay the course and obey the instructions; we understood the assignment.

One specific incident with a longtime member initiated the resurrection of a daunting past of abuse and trauma which sparked the *"caged bird singing"* season in my life. During this season, I was this beautiful, caged bird, singing melodic tunes while being admired by onlookers who perceived that I had it all together. However, my truth was that inside, I was miserably crying out to be freed from oppression and demons from a distant past. It was here that I learned, after years of verbal, mental, physical, and emotional abuse, that I was sadly mistaken for believing I had been fully freed. I also thought that by forgiving my abusers, I had moved on. Boy was I wrong!

In my first marriage, I experienced extensive bouts of physical abuse to deep humiliation, both publicly and privately. Although I was physically removed from harm's way, I somehow remained emotionally attached to familiarity and levels of comfort from those who handled me in ways of humiliation, both publicly and privately. These familiar patterns or "familiar spirits" can be used by the enemy to draw you back into a vicious cycle; used to keep you bound to an unhealthy past. It was not until six years later when we were released from the ministry, that God revealed to me what happened in that season had caused me to be triggered.

The first occurrence happened when I was seated in the main office of the ministry early one Sunday morning handling administrative duties before service. Congregants started to flow in for Sunday School and I greeted them as they came in. One member indicated that she needed to talk with me after Sunday School, and I replied to her, "Yes, of course." The member then circled back with a sense of urgency and entered the office where I was seated, as her need to talk could not be prolonged. The tone in which I was addressed was not only rude and disrespectful, but it also reeked of confrontation and deeply rooted bitterness. I was in complete shock at the entire scene unfolding before my eyes.

I listened and calmly responded by acknowledging the concerns and expressing hopefulness that we could resolve whatever discomforts that were being experienced. It was as if my response added fuel to the fire, and it was also the moment I realized that no matter what I said, it would not bring peace or resolution.

It was here that the Holy Spirit revealed to me that this was an attack directly from an enemy who would use anyone who allowed it to. The individual was not even herself at this moment. It was as if I was encountering someone off the street who was ready to square up. I was in disbelief and completely caught off guard. The "choice words" from the member began to flow and escalate quickly. So much so, that my predecessor/leader came from her office to intervene and diffuse what was unfolding in the House of God. The member finally ceased after she let loose everything in her mind and in her heart, and on to service we went, business as usual. When my husband got news of what had transpired, he was just as confused and upset as I was.

It was a series of occurrences after this incident that caused the triggering to intensify. In this instance, my predecessor basically debriefed me privately and unsupportively told me that I mishandled the situation by completely backing down and showing weakness during the confrontation. I was confused and outdone considering God had previously delivered me from a long journey of anger-management and physical fighting. While I thought I was winning by not responding to my flesh, my leader whom I looked up to, indicated I had failed. I spent many days replaying the incident, in my head, trying to make sense of it. I came up with nothing.

Next, my predecessor reached out during the month of the same member's birthday and decided to recruit me to pick out a special gift for the very person I felt had wronged me. I honored the request from a place of obedience, so I thought and picked out a very beautiful gift for the member. The gift was ordered, purchased, and presented by my predecessor as if she handpicked it herself. It wasn't until this moment that I started to feel very awkward, questioning the motives and intentions of my leader. This experience triggered feelings all too familiar that had been lying dormant within me for many years. The mere act of what was considered "character building" was somehow waking up the spirit of humiliation from my past. The member eventually fell under conviction and publicly apologized to me and asked for forgiveness. This was a true instance of God revealing himself in a situation while vindicating His child. It was also a huge win in the Spirit.

The second trigger came much later. Ironically, it was closer to the time of our release. It occurred on a Sunday in October which happened to be on my birthday. My normal Sunday duty on this day was to deliver the weekly announcements. However, I was quickly informed upon arrival that there would be no announcements on this particular Sunday. I immediately complied and thought nothing of it. Towards the end of service, the designated moderator for the week called on me to make the announcements as she normally would. Apparently, she had not been advised of the sudden change of service. I discreetly shook my head back and forth to signal to her that I would not be making announcements. Suddenly, my leader came marching down the center aisle loudly saying, "Nope, no announcements today". I sank down in my seat embarrassed at the attention that was being publicly drawn to a drastic change in the weekly routine.

Everyone was looking around questioning what was going on. My husband who was in his normal posture after preaching, down on his knees praying, rose off his knees during the confusion. Being the shepherd of the house, he purposely came to the podium after praying and stated, "I have an important announcement… On this very day in October of 1971, a very special woman was born, and that woman is my wife, and today I honor and celebrate her…". The church fell silent as everyone looked on in shock and disbelief as to what was happening, wondering how my birthday acknowledgment was missed. The embarrassment I felt, at that moment, was beyond measure. In addition, my husband was visibly upset about the unfolding scene as birthdays were routinely celebrated in this ministry and remain a huge part of its tradition.

It was a combination of this entire experience, along with members coming up to me apologizing for not acknowledging their "First Lady" on her birthday, that kicked the spirit of humiliation into overdrive. My flesh wanted to run out of the building and wait in the car. This also created flashbacks of public humiliation experienced from past relationships and from childhood. My desire was for the day to just be over. Someone out of sympathy ran out and got a greeting card that was presented to me with a Walmart gift card during the membership meeting held that afternoon.

Fortunately, after being released from the ministry, I was blessed beyond measure to be connected to one of the greatest mentors, prayer warriors, and prophetically anointed women of God who not only coached me but was in sync with the Holy Spirit and effortlessly walked in a place of obedience and submission when it comes to hearing from God. My mentor listened to me and picked up on the need for my deliverance through what I had shared. She was patient, understanding, and eloquently graced with the gifts of correction and guidance through love. Precisely, when I reflected on some of my personal experiences, within the ministry in my sessions, I was able to see the connections and similarities between those experiences and my past. It was revealed to me, at that moment, that the enemy will and can use those who were meant to embrace you, to take you back to eerily familiar places from your past that specifically resurrect old wounds. In this case, it was a past that was deeply connected to the spirit of humiliation. Humiliation is biblically defined as rejection and suffering that Jesus suffered and accepted. This experience, when paired with humanistic experiences of embarrassment, can produce shame that can be severely damaging when endured during any season in our lives. The weightiness of shame is a very heavy load and because we are not Christ, we are not able to endure what Christ has endured.

It was also at this moment I realized that although I had physically been removed from abusive situations of my past and had forgiven my abusers, there were still remnants of the pain from old wounds waiting to be resurrected. It is here that I learned there are different levels of bondage. It was as though I experienced only a taste of freedom by forgiving and letting go of my past which was an outer layer of bondage. The Holy Spirit revealed there was also an inner layer of bondage. It is here that I recognized and acknowledged that I was indeed a caged bird singing. This is a place where people can see you and maybe even admire you for what appears to be your strength and beauty. This is also a place in which the beautiful song you are singing represents an outward cry for help because this place lacks true freedom. Freedom that can only be obtained through Christ and walked out by the presence of His Holy Spirit. It is also here we experience inner healing and full deliverance that completely exposes and uproots any residues from our past. It is here that we can overcome such strongholds.

After going through my own deliverance, it was time for God to heal my marriage. Unfortunately, subtle attempts were made to create division in our marriage through the ministry God had entrusted us with together. It was made clear upon our arrival that God specifically called my husband and me to walk in ministry together. My husband was called to shepherd, pastor, and preach, while I was called to serve women and girls. I was gifted in the prophetic, organizational leadership, and administration. Much more than a caged bird singing.

Within the six years spent in this season, my husband was accepted, honored, and elevated while I was silenced. I was specifically told I was not a pastor and was ignored by leadership when sharing spiritual callings and gifts. I must admit this was a very difficult time in the marriage, which continuously suffered from attacks of the enemy by way of leadership. This included a process of me being gradually excluded from services, prayer, or leadership opportunities. In one instance, a co-pastor who was new to the ministry with no prior experience pastoring, was appointed to work alongside my husband without his knowledge. Considering we had never endured such divisiveness from any outside sources, this was unexpected, surprising, and devastating. Once God released us from the ministry to plant elsewhere, there was a great work of healing that involved the restoration of the marriage and the ministry for my husband and me. It is here we sought wise counsel and mentoring from spiritual leadership that was nonjudgmental, nonbiased, seasoned in marriage and ministry, and versed in sound doctrine. All the said elements were required for complete restoration due to spiritual, emotional, and marital fragility. The matters at hand were indeed matters of the heart and soul. I am forever grateful to my childhood Pastor who poured into us at this crucial time. I truly thank God for the ongoing support of spiritual leaders appointed by God to guide us through.

I would like to leave you with a few things to remember:

- First, never get comfortable and underestimate the enemy. He is cunning, meticulous, and he does not play fair. We must always, even in our healing, be careful of his attacks and devices. We must also be on guard and prepared for battle through warfare. Ephesians 6:12 states, *"For we wrestle not against flesh and blood, but against principalities, against powers, against the rulers of the darkness of this world, against spiritual wickedness in high places."* The enemy can show up any place at any given time, unannounced and even undetected. Therefore, we cannot go into warfare and battles unequipped and unarmed. We must prepare for battle, at any time and in any place. This includes the House of Prayer. This strategy requires an active prayer life and to be fully dressed in the full armour of God in our daily walk.

Finally, my brethren, be strong in the Lord, and in the power of his might. Put on the whole armour of God, that ye may be able to stand against the wiles of the devil. For we wrestle not against flesh and blood, but against principalities, against powers, against the rulers of the darkness of this world, against spiritual wickedness in high places. Wherefore take unto you the whole armour of God, that ye may be able to withstand in the evil day, and having done all, to stand. Stand therefore, having your loins girt about with truth, and having on the breastplate of righteousness; And your feet shod with the preparation of the gospel of peace; Above all, taking the shield of faith, wherewith ye shall be able to quench all the fiery darts of the wicked. And take the helmet of salvation, and the sword of the Spirit, which is the word of God: Praying always with all prayer and supplication in the Spirit and watching thereunto with all perseverance and supplication for all saints. Ephesians 6:10-18 KJV

☐ Next, never let the sting of your past predicate your future. There is healing, restoration, and deliverance in and through you! Sometimes, we may not understand the pain of a current circumstance or season, but we must know that God is likely up to something bigger. In most cases it is not about us, but ultimately about those who will be healed and set free by our testimony and truth. Never be afraid to bless someone with your story. Although we may experience drought at times, it is only for a season. Where God guides, He will provide! *And the LORD will continually guide you, and satisfy your soul in scorched and dry places, and give strength to your bones; And you will be like a watered garden, and like a spring of water whose waters do not fail.* Isaiah 58:11AMP

☐ Lastly, your "true" restoration is no longer bound to your past. In this process, each layer of the enemy's plots and plans are exposed and cast down to an unfruitful place. It is here that true freedom in Christ is experienced. Isaiah 43:18-19 (NIV) *Forget the former things; do not dwell on the past. See, I am doing a new thing! Now it springs up; do you not perceive it? I am making a way in the wilderness and streams in the wasteland.*

Father God,

In the mighty and matchless name of Jesus, I pray right now that every dry season experienced by each person reading this will be restored and replenished in all ways, from this day forward. I pray that all attacks of the enemy will be fully exposed for what they are, no matter the source. I pray that each layer of hurt, pain, and suffering experienced from their past be completely healed, leaving no layer unturned and unaddressed. I bind and take authority over the spirits of manipulation, intimidation, and control. I pray that each woman who is called to serve in ministry alongside her husband be girted up and equipped daily with the full armor of God. I also pray that every caged bird singing will be set free to carry out the assignment and the commission in a place of freedom and confidence in you Oh Lord. I pray that Holy boldness encompasses every testimony lying dormant, igniting the courage to come forth In Jesus' name, waiting to be a blessing to another. I declare and decree each of you be like a watered garden and a spring of Your true and living word that never fails.

In Jesus name,
Amen

If you or anyone that you know is experiencing Domestic Violence Text BEGIN at 88788 or call 1-800-7233.

SALUTING BLACK WOMEN PREACHERS
WHO LIVED THE CALL

The biographical sketches are quoted directly from Candice Benbow's article, "Black women preachers who changed-and are changing-history" (Benbow, 2022). They each reflect historical witness of the resilience and current expression of a courage that must be fueled by the Holy Sprit's power and presence.

The Rev. Raquel S. Lettsome, Ph.D. - A nationally renowned preacher and biblical scholar, Lettsome is the founder of RSL Ministries, where she works with faith leaders and laity, offering courses in exegesis, sermon preparation, and ways to build better bible studies. Lettsome holds the distinction of being the first African-American to receive a Ph.D. in New Testament from Princeton Theological Seminary and is currently a Visiting Scholar of the New Testament at Eden Theological Seminary.

Dr. Melva L. Sampson - Sampson is the creator and curator of Pink Robe Chronicles (PRC), a digital hush harbor that centers faith and spirituality utilizing the womanist tenets of redemptive self-love, critical engagement, radical subjectivity, and traditional communalism with a focus on Black women. PRC streams live on Facebook and YouTube every Sunday at 8:00 am EST. Sampson is also the author of the forthcoming Going Live!: Black Women's Proclamation in the Digital Age.

Chapter 14

Rev. Kimberly Waldon

Rev. Kimberly Waldon

Pastor Kimberly Waldon, a native of Detroit, Michigan, resides in Raleigh, North Carolina. She is married to Pastor Ronald P. Waldon, Jr. and the proud mother of Ronald P. Waldon, III.

Pastor Kimberly is a graduate of Madonna University (Livonia, Michigan) where she received her B.S. Degree in Business Administration. She received her Master of Science Degree in International Administration from Central Michigan University (Mt. Pleasant, Michigan) and Master of Divinity Degree from Shaw University Divinity School, Raleigh, North Carolina.

Pastor Kimberly began her ministry journey in 1996 and served as Youth Director at New Liberty Baptist Church, Detroit, Michigan (1996-2006) and Youth Ministry Director at Macedonia New Life Church, Raleigh, North Carolina (2006-2009). She has also served in other ministry roles and settings at the District, State, and National Baptist Congress levels.

Pastor Kimberly received her license to preach the gospel in October 2013 and was ordained in November 2018. She served as the first woman Moderator (2019-2021) and Board Chair of New Home and Durham Missionary Baptist Association, Durham, North Carolina 128-year-old District Association. She has also served in leadership roles including Christian Education Director, Youth Director, Teen Girl Director/Advisor, and Women's Ministry Director.

In March 2021, she launched Kimberly Waldon Ministries, an outreach ministry focused on spiritual growth, ministry leadership, and personal development of men and women through classes, training, and mentoring/coaching sessions.

On April 3, 2022, Kimberly and her husband, Ronald accepted the call to serve as pastors of New Jerusalem Community Church, Durham North Carolina.

Pastor Kimberly is a servant with a heart for God and leads God's people, through the Spirit, towards spiritual formation and transformation.

For speaking, preaching, and conference engagements, please email: kimberlywaldonministries@gmail.com.

Finally Revealed...
Journeys of Grace

"Be he said to me, 'My grace is sufficient for you, for my power is made perfect in weakness." 2 Corinthians 12:9

I am grateful that God has given me supernational strength to endure and overcome many obstacles in my life. The journeys that God has allowed me to experience have been transformative and my capacity to receive His will for my life has increased. In fact, every journey has been a discovery of God's grace at so many levels. 2 Corinthians 12:9 has been my constant reminder that I need God in every journey in my life and that I cannot do anything without His grace. I have come to realize I am Graced for the Journey, and that God is my Source of Sufficiency.

The Beginning...

It all began at age 17. I was asked to be the speaker for our Sunday morning Graduation Day. At the time, I was thrilled to have been selected to share to the graduating class of 1986 and to the congregation of the church. Little did I know that God was preparing me to serve in pulpit preaching ministry. That opportunity led to several other speaking engagements.

During this time, in the mid 1980's, the Baptist church experienced a rise in women preachers. In fact, the most frequent topic of discussion among the churches was centered around women preachers and their call to preach. I was raised during this era when women were prohibited from preaching. Women were allowed to speak from the floor but not from the pulpit.

As the invitations increased to share in ministry, I was challenged by this theology that shaped the mindsets of many. I can recall having this discussion with my mother, a strong woman of faith, who served as one of the Sunday School teachers at our church. Although my mother grew up with this theology, she admits that after in-depth study and prayer, the Holy Spirit had given her a new revelation of women and their calling to serve as preachers and perform pastoral roles in ministry. She has always encouraged me to exhibit that "I Can Do All Things Through Christ" spirit and to "Move Forward Trusting God." I must admit that both, my mother and father were strong supporters of me.

Fast forward to 2012, while in the office of my spiritual father in the ministry and my husband, I accepted the call to preach. It was soon after the call, I realized that ministry was not easy. Just like everyone else, your role in ministry doesn't exempt you from dealing with your own emotional, spiritual, physical, mental, and financial issues, But God!

Grace of Sustainability

As a leader in ministry, I have trusted the sustaining grace of God. The grace that matures us and gives us the drive to press forward. My husband and I have been married for 29 years and served in ministry together for over 25 years. In our early years, we served in youth ministry together. When my husband accepted his first pastorate in 2008, I was then identified as the "Pastor's Wife or the First Lady" where I served to support various ministries under his leadership. My husband encouraged me to use my spiritual gifts to serve God in ministry. This role was truly a fulfilling one, but also came with some challenges; there were issues that didn't sit well with some church leadership and congregants. I can recall at a church meeting that my husband chaired, he was giving his vision to the church. He shared that he wanted me to serve in leadership roles in the areas of Christian Education and Women's ministry. After my husband had given his direction, one of the deacons raised his hand and said, "We don't want our First Lady to serve. We just want her to sit on the front row and look pretty." His suggestion didn't sit well with my spirit. It was at that moment, that I knew that God was challenging and stretching me. I also knew that I had to define my role as First Lady. I conveyed to the deacon and others in the room that *'God has called me to serve and share the gifts that He has given to me with His people. Being a First Lady will not change my passion and willingness to serve.'* It was this stereotype and many other trials that I experienced being married to the pastor.

Another interesting experience in my journey was at one of the former churches where my husband served as pastor. I attended a leadership meeting at the church that was led by the Deacons. All leaders of ministries were requested to attend this meeting. At the time, I served as the leader of the Women's Ministry. It was my third year serving in this role and I have attended these leadership meetings in the past. Fifteen minutes after the meeting started, the deacon stood and said that I had to leave the meeting. To not cause a scene and to respect my husband's position as the pastor, I handled the situation in a Christ-like character and left the meeting. I was not only confused, but I was truly frustrated. My husband did not attend this meeting, but I called him once I left. He immediately reached out to the Deacons and was told because I was not "a member" of the church, I was not allowed to attend the meeting. It was evident to me, after two years of attending these leadership meetings, that this had nothing to do with membership. I believe that they were intimidated by my leadership influence in the ministry. It was their way of slowing down ministry progress and my leadership authority to satisfy their own insecurities and traditions. The culture of the church limited my full expression of ministry gifts to the congregation. We had hungry women who embraced the vision, yearned for fresh revelation, and had a strong desire to grow.

I must add that there were good moments that encouraged me while in the role of First Lady. I had the awesome opportunity to mentor women, cast vision and see the transformative work of the Holy Spirit in many of the women's lives in our churches.

Grace of Frustration

In 2016, I was appointed to serve as Board Direct Chair, a new position within our district association. This district association was 125 years old. My role was to chair the board meetings, ensure that churches were in compliance with the association's bylaws, and be of support to the Moderator. At the time, this district association had fourteen active churches. I took office during a time when the member churches and leaders had concerns with previous leadership, lack of member pastor involvement and engagement, failure to clearly establish the purpose of the association, concerns about the needed repair of the building structure, and the financial concerns of paying high property taxes. During my tenure as Board Chair, we were able to build a core team and the association thrived through new leadership. Under my leadership, we successfully addressed and resolved concerns. I served in the role for two years.

When my tenure as Board Chair ended, I was nominated to serve as the District Association Moderator. After much prayer, I decided to accept the nomination. I must share that when I accepted the nomination, I had not been ordained, nor pastored a church. I was the first female to be elected Moderator of the District Association. This raised some concerns among pastors who felt that I was not qualified for this position. On the day of the election, there were only two nominees. I was one of two from the District Association. Right before the election process, there was a question raised from the floor. In fact, the question was posed by a member from my former church. This individual questioned my lack of qualifications to serve in this role. The current Moderator, at the time, responded to this member's question and made it clear to her that my nomination was in order. It was unusual but it was in order.

After the voting process was completed, I was elected as the Moderator by an overwhelming response. In fact, I was the first female to hold this position in a district of male pastors. I can remember seeing the faces of many of my sisters in the faith, being surprised but also encouraged by the outcome. This was a historical moment in the life of this district association. I received congratulatory calls and text messages from members of the district churches but very few from the district pastors. My opponent was disgruntled and a few days after the vote, he requested a recount of the votes. The Board of Directors honored his request for a recount, but the results did not change. Needless to say, this pastor's participation ceased during my tenure.

When I got into office I, along with my team, began to do the work of rebuilding our district association. I began with the pastors of the churches. I called each of them to set up an introductory meeting. Out of 14 pastors, only 6 pastors responded to my request to meet with them. When I followed up with them, they did not respond. It was evident that they had issues with me being a female leading this association.

As Moderator, in efforts to build relationships, I was intentional in attending Pastoral Anniversaries and Church Anniversaries of our member churches. One incident, I can recall, I arrived at the church during a pastor's anniversary. I told the usher I was there and would like to do a special presentation to the pastor. I was escorted to the front of the church by one of the ushers. The pastor overlooked me during the entire service. It was not until the usher told him that I was there, that he recognized me and allowed me to do the special presentation. It was this incident and others that frustrated me while in this role. God's presence and guidance kept me through it all. I effectively served my term as Moderator for three years.

This grace of frustration revealed to me that my battles are inevitable. God's grace picked me up and reminded me that in this journey I am not alone. It's through God's grace that allowed me to move forward not in my own strength but in His strength.

Grace of the Call

When God placed this calling on my life, He gave me the grace to be and do what He has called me to do. Paul wrote in 1 Corinthians 15:10, "By the grace of God I am what I am: and His grace which was bestowed upon me was not in vain." I hone in on this scripture because it is a constant reminder to me that in every journey, God is equipping me to fulfill my purpose by His grace.

In 2021, I along with my husband, accepted the call to serve as co-pastors of our current church. This is my first pastorate. For many who do not know, co-pastoring is where two individuals, or in our case, husband and wife, equally share a pastoral role.

For me, this journey has been both a blessing, but it has also come with some challenges as it relates to others in the ministry comprehending this concept of leadership. For my husband and me, co-pastoring is ideal. We both have full-time careers outside of our vocational calling. This pastorate assignment gives us the opportunity to share the ministry responsibilities. My husband supports me to the fullest. We both share in the preaching and teaching components of ministry without difficulties. We serve communion together. We discuss prior to meetings with our congregants regarding who will chair meetings. We apply intentional efforts to be on one accord relative to communication. I must say that we don't always agree or have the same thoughts, but we find a way to work things out as partners in the ministry. Our approach to ministry is all about completing and not competing. Our church appreciates both our gifts and the different perspectives that we offer in our role.

The challenge of co-pastoring has not necessarily been from disciples of our church but from others who tend to view pastoral leadership from a patriarchal lens. This continues to be a struggle in the Black Church. Despite the acceptance of my pastoral, role in some ministry contexts, patriarchy continues to be the elephant in the room. More often than not, people (men, as well as, women) look at my husband as the sole leader and not us as co-equals. I can't tell you how many times people would come up to us and address my husband as "Pastor" and me as the "Pastor's Wife" or "First Lady."

The patriarchal culture has driven me, and perhaps many other women, to work harder, speak up more often, and do more in an effort to prove ourselves. Recently, I was asked to render prayer at my cousin's wedding and the minister addressed me as 'Kimberly.' I kindly told him to address me as 'Reverend Kimberly Waldon.' Trust me, I am not really stuck on titles, but I believe that in public spaces and within certain audiences, I should have the same respect as my male peers.

Although this is discouraging and draining mentally, emotionally, and spiritually, I have come to understand that ultimately my purpose is to bring God glory and make impact in His Kingdom. God called me to this ministry "to go and proclaim", I did not call myself.

Grace of Healing

In December 2022, while a caregiver for my husband after a tragic car accident, I was diagnosed with breast cancer. In order for the cancer to not spread, it was necessary for me to begin the cancer treatments immediately. This diagnosis took me by surprise. In fact, I was so shaken by the news that there were no tears, only laments of disbelief. I asked the questions, *"Why me?"* and *"Why now?"* The news had my mind exploring many thoughts. I had thoughts of my mortality, family care, and church-work-life impact.

Because my husband was still recovering from his accident, I was solely responsible for leading the church for two and half months while I had undergone surgery and radiation treatments. This included preparing weekly Sunday messages and Bible Study, preaching and teaching, and overseeing and providing pastoral care and counseling to our church members. This time in my life, I would best describe from Ecclesiastes 8:17 as my *"under the sun"* season. Life changes go on "under the sun." I had to accept and embrace this season of my life with its challenges and trust God and His wisdom.

I thank God for our ministers who graciously provided pulpit support during this time. While this was an unfortunate time, I believe God used this moment in my life as a healing blessing.

I made the decision not to share my diagnosis with many people. My diagnosis was only shared with my circle of close family, friends, and prayer warriors. I did this to eliminate the focused attention from others on my diagnosis and how that would affect me and the church. During this time, it was necessary to avoid all distractions and to stay focused. I had to trust, for myself, that God would bear the weight of everything I was experiencing. I had to exercise my faith knowing that God had everything in control. The blessing for me was I drew on Proverbs 3:5-6, "Trust in the Lord with all your heart and lean not on your own understanding; in all your ways acknowledge him, and he will make your paths straight." This gave me daily healing to my soul and spirit. I am thankful to God for His healing grace to me physically, emotionally, and spiritually. By the grace of God, I am now a Cancer Survivor.

The work of ministry is never-ending and not easy. The journey comes with some unwelcome, unfortunate, and hurtful circumstances. As a woman in ministry, I had to put some non-negotiables in place to help me endure, grow, and experience freedom. A wise person once said, "You can't pour from an empty cup." It was necessary that I move from people and spaces that tainted my spirit and connect with people and outlets that offered fueling and renewal. I learned to pray without ceasing, trust God, and love even when it was hard.

I thank God for my journey and His plan on my life. Although I experienced some challenges in ministry, the call and the privilege to serve is rewarding. It is rewarding to see the graces of God manifested in His people. God has graced me with a calling to make a difference in the world, despite the pain. At the end of the day, my spiritual goal is to "...keep my eyes on the prize" (Philippians 3:14) so God is glorified!

Chapter 15

Rev. Dr. Karen Wicker

Rev. Dr. Karen Wicker

Reverend Dr. Karen Moore Wicker was born in Washington, D.C. to Geneva H. Moore and the late Leonard Moore. She graduated from the National Cathedral School and then earned her Bachelor of Arts in Biology from the University of Pennsylvania. She graduated with honors from Meredith College with a master's degree in business administration. She continued her education and graduated from Shaw University Divinity School, earning a Master of Divinity degree. She earned the Doctor of Ministry degree at Hood Theological Seminary in Salisbury, North Carolina, with a concentration in Pastoral Theology and Care. She has also completed Clinical Pastoral Education at Rex Hospital in Raleigh, North Carolina.

Dr. Wicker has formerly served as Associate Minister, Youth Pastor, Vacation Bible School Coordinator, member of the Prison Ministry, and High School Sunday School Teacher. She also serves as a Professor of Denominational History, Polity, and Doctrine at the Heritage School of Biblical and Theological Studies in Raleigh, North Carolina. She has been an adjunct professor at the Triangle School of Theology. She also serves as a mentor to doctoral students preparing for their dissertation and defense. Dr. Wicker is employed as the Manager of County Engagement at a local health insurance company.

In the community, she has served as a Pastoral Care Volunteer at the Christian United Outreach Center. She is currently a commissioner at the Sanford Housing Authority Board and is also the former secretary of the Board of Directors of the Bread Basket in Sanford, North Carolina.

Rev. Wicker is a charter member of the Sandhills Alumnae Chapter of Delta Sigma Theta Sorority, Inc., where she has held many leadership positions including: Chaplain, Treasurer, Chair of Policies and Procedures, Physical and Mental Health, and Educational Development committees. She is also a member of the South Atlantic Regional Chaplain's Council for the sorority.

Rev. Wicker and her husband, Willie Wicker, reside in Sanford, North Carolina. She has one son Steven, and a stepdaughter, Shonta. Rev. Wicker enjoys traveling and spending time with her family. She also loves the challenge of crossword puzzles, sudoku, and mahjong.

One of her favorite scriptures can be found in Micah 6:8 where it says "*…and what doth the Lord require of thee, but to do justly, and to love mercy, and to walk humbly with thy God?*"

To God be the glory!

Invited to the Party, But No One Asked Me to Dance!

*Diversity is being invited to the party.
Inclusion is being invited to dance.*
— Verna Myers

Rejection is a part of life. It helps us to see opportunities for improvement and encourages us to aim higher. It forces us to look at ourselves, but also creates an opportunity to see ourselves from the vantage point of someone else. With maturity, we realize that the perceptions of others, depending on their motives, past experiences, and biases, may be accurate or completely wrong.

My parents sacrificed much to make sure I had the best education. It was a top priority in my house. As it was time to prepare to start the college application process, everyone in my class was required to meet with the college counselor. I had heard my classmates who wanted to continue in single-sex learning, talk about attending Smith and Wellesley. Others who wanted to stay closer to home were choosing Georgetown, Trinity or Catholic University. Some wanted to explore not only diverse curricula but also other areas of the country and were bound for Washington state. I am not sure when it happened, but I had my heart set on attending an Ivy League school. In my mind, it was the best and that's what I wanted. So, during my appointment with the college counselor, I expressed my interest in the Ivies. She quickly dissuaded me as if to indicate that was not a viable possibility. Instead, she said I should apply to "safety" schools, pointing out the local HBCU. I was offended. Hadn't I completed the same course of study as the majority of my classmates? What made them more suitable for the colleges they wanted to attend? I decided to apply anyway in spite of what she said. After all, it wasn't her money for the application fees, and no one said I had to take her advice. In addition to several other schools, I applied to five in the Ivies. I was offered admission to three of them and ultimately attended the University of Pennsylvania. We had to report to the school all the applications and outcomes and our final choices were posted on the bulletin board for the entire school to see. I don't remember ever having another conversation with the counselor and so there were certainly no congratulatory words. This was probably the beginning of my "well, I'll show you" attitude.

I clearly remember working in corporate America trying to get promoted and earn more money. I became aware of an MBA program that allowed students to attend classes at night, so this was exactly what I needed. By now, I was a single parent of an elementary school-aged little boy. How would I manage that? I was able to get the help of a dear friend who would pick him up from school, give him dinner, and help with homework. After class, I picked my son up from her house, went home to check homework, gave him a bath, and off to bed. Then, it was time to do my homework. As if that wasn't enough, we were required to alert our direct manager about our intent to attend school so that she could approve the tuition refund request. I took her the card and explained what I had planned. Her words to me were, "Oh no, you don't want to do that!" It was happening again. I looked at her strangely, but based on previous conversations I was not surprised. Why was this encouraged for my majority counterparts - especially men? It was now imperative that I not only attend but earn that degree. When I took my grade report showing that I had earned an A in my first class, she was shocked and reluctantly signed for my reimbursement. This scene repeated itself every semester for three years until I finally completed my degree and graduated with honors.

Rejection can make us better but can also make us bitter and crush our self-esteem.

And then it happened...

I had been wondering what the Lord really wanted from my life. I was a solid believer, faithful, and followed the rules, but I knew more was required. Serving on committees, counting money and reading the morning announcements in service was not fulfilling even though it was necessary work.

On a blustery November day, I was visiting a friend in the hospital during my lunch break. I had visited before, but this day was different and would turn out to be a pivotal point in my life. The call came from the Lord to serve. It was so clear and unmistakable. As I went back to my car, I called my husband and, with immense excitement, exclaimed that I now knew what the Lord required of me. After the initial euphoria wore off, then the panic set in. How in the world would I begin? After much prayer, I applied to seminary, and with the help and support of my pastor, I began the journey of preparation for ministry.

Seminary was full of surprises. Extreme highs and devastating lows were the order of the day along with immense amounts of reading and research. I formed several relationships, a few of which would become lifelong friends and colleagues. However, it was during my time at Shaw that I started to notice vast differences between my educational prowess and that of some of my male counterparts. Some of the males were already pastors and bragged about the sizes of their churches and their tenure in the pulpit. Others reflected on their doting congregations. I already felt inadequate as one who had not yet even preached her initial sermon and was not sure I belonged there. However, some seemed to lack what I characterized as basic reading, writing and comprehension skills that made me wonder how they had been accepted to a graduate degree program. Nevertheless, I continued and did my best, graduating with honors. For some reason, I expected that my new ministerial colleagues - both male and female - would grant me an opportunity to serve at their churches at some time in the future. After all, we had all participated in late-night study groups, note exchanges, and even provided support and encouragement when needed. In most cases, I was wrong.

After graduation, I was able to serve some at my church and was granted the opportunity to become the Youth Pastor. I was able to develop my own curriculum and shape the ministry, as it was the first at this church. Developing policies and procedures, an order of service, and incorporating Holy Communion (after ordination) was exciting and fulfilling. I formed a bond with many of the young people in the ministry and gave them opportunities to serve as well. For several years, I was also able to direct the Vacation Bible School program with a special focus on the music ministry. One of the most exciting parts of this was engaging the surrounding community; inviting them to participate in all our church had to offer. This would then lead to the inception of the community youth Bible study held at the local Boys and Girls Club where we served dinner and taught approximately forty children each week. What a blessing. My pastor was a constant supporter of this program.

Now as the years started to tick by, it was apparent that invitations to preach at a Women's Day or Mother's Day service might come, but only an occasional Sunday morning invitation. I invited some of my seminary colleagues to preach at our services and welcomed them. The limitations were becoming more evident.

I started to ask myself, "What is missing? Is there something else I need to do?" The achievement of the Master of Divinity degree had taught me one thing - the more I studied, the more I realized what I did not know. I loved being in school; earning the Doctor of Ministry degree seemed like a logical next step. That is exactly what I did. Again, I gained a couple of lifelong friends and while those who could have provided ministry opportunities were satisfied working with me in class, it stopped there.

PF Flyers ®

As a little girl, there was a sneaker brand called PF Flyers ®. My parents had bought me a pair of these popular green sneakers. Their slogan was that PF flyers would make you "run faster and jump higher". There was no one who could convince me that once I laced them up, I couldn't do just as the motto said! But as someone who was about six years old, I did not know that motto would become what ministry looked like for me and many other women like me. It was indeed true that I had to "run faster and jump higher" than my male counterparts just to get recognized. It wasn't fair and the aura of the patriarchy just seemed to get bigger.

Separate But Equal

So now what was the problem? I now had four sets of letters (degrees) behind my name. I had done all that was asked of me and pursued my ministry work with excellence. Any time I was granted an opportunity, I ensured I was prepared and took each preaching or teaching engagement very seriously. I was equal on paper but continued to be treated as a separate entity.

Bias - Conscious or Unconscious?

Biases - we all have them whether we admit it or not. There are some that are part of our upbringing and are a result of our lived experiences, while others are intentional and explicit. I would like to explore three different types of biases for this writing.

First, let us define conscious versus unconscious bias:

Conscious Bias (also known as explicit bias) refers to the prejudiced beliefs or attitudes one has towards a person or group on a conscious level. Explicit attitudes are feelings and thoughts that one deliberately believes and can consciously document.

Unconscious biases are social stereotypes about certain groups of people that individuals form outside their own conscious awareness. Everyone holds unconscious beliefs about various social and identity groups, and these biases stem from one's tendency to organize social worlds by categorizing.

It is important to note that biases, conscious or unconscious, are not limited to ethnicity and race. Though racial bias and discrimination are well documented, biases may exist toward any social group. One's age, gender, gender identity, physical abilities, religion, sexual orientation, weight, and many other characteristics are subject to bias.[1]

Confirmation Bias

Confirmation Bias is the tendency to favor information that aligns with our existing beliefs or attitudes. It includes associating stereotypes or attitudes towards groups without being consciously aware. Just because we are not consciously aware of biases, does not mean our actions don't have real impacts. Unchecked, biases can lead to detrimental forms of racism.

Just because we're not consciously aware of biases doesn't mean we're off the hook. Just because we're not consciously aware, doesn't mean there's nothing we can do about it. Just because we are not consciously aware of biases doesn't mean it's not pervasive. We are still accountable for our (un)learning, learning, interrogating, and changing these biases. Biases are inevitable, BUT it does not mean they're not immovable.[2]

---

[1] https://ecampusontario.pressbooks.pub/universaldesign/chapter/uncovering-unconscious-bias/#:~:text

[2] https://libraryguides.saic.edu/learn_unlearn/foundations6#:~:text=Conscious Bias

Groupthink

Groupthink is a type of unconscious bias where people want to achieve group consensus. People will adopt the thoughts and opinions of the group while setting aside their personal beliefs and values. Groupthink is present in many aspects but is mostly found to occur during decision-making processes. The most damaging effect of groupthink is the pressure on group members to conform to the group and form a consensus that results in the exclusion of other ideas, perspectives, talents, skills, and thoughts. Remote collaboration requires a diversity of thought, experiences, and backgrounds.

The Oppressors

Oppression takes many forms and, as African Americans, we are painfully familiar with many types of oppression. Some versions are more subtle, while others are overt and brutal. Oppression may also have a numbing effect on some who have just decided that they are content with the status quo and the existing power system and hierarchy. Oppression can either make its victim surrender and render them powerless to change their plight or it can make them fight to be free. Realizing that it was the Lord who called me to service and not any human, I have chosen the latter. In this context, I define an Oppressor as one who, for a variety of reasons, does not acknowledge, affirm, or support my calling and tries to negate any contribution I may have to further the kingdom of God. For some oppressors, this is absolutely a conscious and calculated choice. They are free to operate in the system to which they have become accustomed and is comfortable for them. Oppressors may incorporate conscious or unconscious biases or both in their formulation of ideas characterizing what is acceptable or valuable.

Present and Prepared

The expression "seat at the table" is often used to describe the environment and operating system in which one must function to be a contributor or a leader. I have devised my own method to measure and determine what type of "seat" I might have at any table given the gender, position, influence, and standing of those already seated. This system allows me to determine in an objective manner how my presence and contribution may be perceived:

1. **Granted a seat at the table.**
   I call this *acceptance*. If I am offered a seat at the table, the other participants, and especially the leader, accept that I am present and prepared even though I might make them uneasy or uncomfortable.

2. **Bringing my own seat to the table.**
   I call this *tolerance*. Room was made for me, no one offered me a seat but allowed me to bring my own chair, demonstrating my willingness and determination to be present in spite of not being welcomed.

3. **Standing in the room around the table.**
   I called this *marginalized*. No chair is available or offered and there is no room for another chair. Clearly, exclusion is the message, and the worth of my contribution and value is diminished. Oppression is at work in full force in this instance and no matter how present or prepared, those at the table ignore you. The level of preparedness, even though it exceeds that of many of those who are seated, is negated.

4. **Bringing my own table and chairs into the room.**
   I call this *expansion*. This creates an atmosphere where I can create my own opportunities as well as open doors for others. At this table, everyone's gift can make room for them because there are enough seats for all who want to gather around the table. There are enough chairs for others to join and no one in the room is intimidated by those who have come to contribute.

Moving Forward

Verna Myers said, "Men are our defaults. What are we afraid of?" My hope for this piece is that some who suffer from unconscious biases will begin to see themselves as products of their environments and endeavor to change their outlooks. I understand that some readers may resolve to stick with their current beliefs, and they have the right to do so. However, it is my duty to walk worthy in the vocation in which I was called and serve God wholeheartedly. To that end, I move forward asking the Lord to create opportunities for me to spread His Word, and He continues to do just that. Whether preaching, writing, teaching, or doing Facebook and YouTube videos, the Gospel message continues to go forth. I sincerely appreciate the men and women who affirm and support women in the ministry and help to remove barriers. Thank you to all those who nurture and teach us as we continue to hone our craft and expand our borders. I am grateful to my husband of almost twenty-five years for his unwavering support and honest assessments. My son is my chief cheerleader. My mom, sister, and brother have been my champions.

There is a place for all of us- not only at the foot of the cross but in the pulpit as well.

Suggested Readings

LaRue, Cleophus ed. *This Is My Story*. Louisville: John Knox Press, 2005.

Lovett, Shauntia, "*Maternal Ministry, Other Mothering, And FindingPower For Women In The Black Church: A Phenomenological Exploration.*" Thesis, Georgia State University, 2014

Mitchell, Ella Pearson ed. *Those Preaching Women, Volume 3*. Valley Forge: Judson Press, 1966.

Myers, V. (2014). How to overcome our biases? Walk boldly toward them. Ted Talk.

Nelms Smarr, Kimberly, Rachelle Disbennett-Lee, and Amy Cooper Hakim. 2018. "*Gender and Race in Ministry Leadership: Experiences of Black Clergywomen*" Religions 9, no. 12: 377.

Palmer, Brittani. *The Truth About Black Women in Ministry*. Sojourners, 2021.

https://sojo.net/articles/truth-about-black-women-ministry
Rudolph, Christine R. *A Different Perspective: Examining Obstacles Faced By Black Clergywomen Through the Lenses of Critical Race Feminism*. The Journal of Value-Based Leadership.

https://scholar.valpo.edu/cgi/viewcontent.cgi?article=1454&context=jvbl

Stewart, Gina M. *We've Got Next*. Chicago: MMGI Books, 2015.

Walker-Barnes, Chanequa. *Too Heavy a Yoke*. Oregon: MMGI Books, 2014.

SALUTING BLACK WOMEN PREACHERS WHO LIVED THE CALL

In addition to the 15 powerful women in this book, *The PreacHER in Her: Living the Call,* there are two women preachers who are notable for their contributions in living the call.

Bishop Vashti Murphy McKenzie was the first Black woman preacher elected as the 117th consecrated bishop of the African Methodist Episcopal (AME) Church.

Dr. Gina Stewart is the first woman elected president of the Lott Carey Baptist Foreign Mission Society and the first female president of a national African American Baptist mission agency or convention, Lott Carey. Dr. Stewart is also the first woman to preach in the National Baptist Joint Board Session.

SALUTING BLACK WOMEN PREACHERS
WHO LIVED THE CALL

References

10th Episcopal District of the AME Church. (2001). *Meet our Bishop*. Retrieved 2015, from Tenth Episcopal District of the African Methodist Episcopal Church: http://www.10thdistrictame.org/bishop.html.

Benbow, Candice Marie. 2022. "Black Women Preachers Who Changed—and Are Changing—History." TheGrio. March 8, 2022. https://thegrio.com/2022/03/08/black-women-preachers-who-changed-history/. Biographical Sketches.

Edwards, Chris. 2024. "PhD Student Gina Stewart Makes Preaching History." Christian Theological Seminary. February 6, 2024. https://www.cts.edu/2024/02/06/phd-student-gina-stewart-makes-preaching-history/.

Lott Carey. (2021). *First woman elected president of United States-based Baptist Group*. Lott Cary, June 23, 2024. https://lottcarey.org/2021/08/first-woman-elected-president-of-united-states-based-baptist-group/.

**THE COLLECTIVE JOURNEYS OF
15 WOMEN IN MINISTRY**

DR. JOE L. STEVENSON

Compilation Visionary:

Rev. Dr. Joe L. Stevenson

Rev. Dr. Joe L. Stevenson

Compilation Visionary, Reverend Dr. Joe L. Stevenson, is a noted theologian, academician, and prognosticator of the gospel. For over 40 years, he has carried the mantle proclaiming the death, resurrection, and ascension of Jesus Christ.

A native of Crawford, Mississippi, Rev. Dr. Joe L. Stevenson first acknowledged God's anointing at an early age. In 1980, Rev. Dr. Stevenson accepted God's calling into ministry and was ordained to preach by Reverend Joe A. Stevenson of St. Joseph Baptist Church in St. Louis, Missouri.

Rev. Dr. Stevenson first pastored the Temple of Faith Missionary Baptist Church in Kansas City, Missouri for six years. During this time, he hosted a full-time Gospel radio ministry. Subsequently, he would go on to serve as pastor of New Liberty Baptist Church in Detroit, Michigan for 16 years as God blessed the ministry to grow from 500 to 1000 disciples. In 2006, Rev. Dr. Stevenson was positioned to lead Macedonia New Life Church in Raleigh, North Carolina where he proudly serves as senior pastor. He considers it to be his assignment to lead this great church in shaping the future of Christ's church. As a church planter, Rev. Dr. Stevenson and Macedonia New Life Church are nurturing Iglesia Hispana Macedonia.

In addition to Rev Dr. Stevenson's full-time ministry at Macedonia New Life Church, he held administrative and teaching positions at the first historically Black institution of higher education in the South, Shaw University. Rev. Dr. Stevenson served as Director of Continuing Education and remains at Shaw University Divinity School as an adjunct associate professor. Rev. Dr. Stevenson has also served as an adjunct professor at Myers Taylor School of Religion, Ashland University, and Ashland Theological Seminary. Academic courses taught by Rev. Dr. Stevenson, include *Pastoral Care, Evangelism, Church Administration, Spiritual Formation, Social Activism, Person in Prayer, and Spiritual Disciplines*. He is the 2021 recipient of the Gus Witherspoon Award in religion and a 2023 recipient of the Community Impact Award from The Northeastern Region of Sigma Gamma Rho Sorority, Inc. and The Middle Eastern Province of Kappa Alpha Psi Fraternity, Inc. In March 2023, he was appointed to serve as Director of the Black Church Leadership Academy at Shaw University.

Rev. Dr. Stevenson is committed to professional, civic, and social organizations. He is the former chairman of Friends of Detroit City Airport and a former Board Member of the Raleigh Urban League. He served as the Second Vice President of the Baptist Missions and Education (B.M.&E.) State Congress of Christian Education, Director of Ushers, and as the Field Missionary for the Prospect District Association of Churches. Currently, Rev. Dr. Stevenson holds a seat on the Board of Directors for LUCC Ltd., and is a member of the Ecumenical Council, National Association for the Advancement of Colored People (NAACP), and his beloved fraternal organization, Kappa Alpha Psi Fraternity, Incorporated.

Rev. Dr. Stevenson earned a Master of Divinity in Pastoral Counseling, Master of Arts, and Doctor of Ministry in Formational Counseling and Pastoral Care from Ashland Theological Seminary of Ashland University, located in Ashland, Ohio. He cites the psalmist David as a favorite biblical reference and adds, much like David, God's light gave him clarity; clarity to seek salvation and in turn, God gave him covering to sustain him throughout all facets of life. Since being selected as a mentor for the Lilly Pastors of Excellence Program in 2003, he shared this mantra to mentor pastors in their professional development for healthier congregations of Jesus Christ. Now, he continues to share the Gospel of Jesus Christ internationally. Rev. Dr. Stevenson toured the Vatican City and Ancient Rome. He has lectured and preached in Lusaka, Ndola, and Sioma, all in Zambia; and in Johannesburg, South Africa, and serves on the advisory committee for the inception of the Shikaru Leadership Academy.

Rev. Dr. Joe Stevenson and his wife, Brenda, a Wake County Public School educator, are blessed to be the proud parents of five children- three sons: LeVaughn, Joseph, and Brennan, and two daughters: Makiea & Briona. They have ten grandchildren – Khloe, Londyn, Victoria, Nora, Michelle, Joey, Kaleb, Micah, Ezra and Aalaya.

Contact Rev. Dr. Joe L. Stevenson:
Website: www.jlstevensonministries.org
Email: drjoestevenson@gmail.com
Phone: 919-618-3447
Social Media:
www.facebook.com/pastorjoe.stevenson
www.linkedin.com/in/dr-joe-stevenson-09812525/

**THE COLLECTIVE JOURNEYS OF
15 WOMEN IN MINISTRY**

DR. JOE L. STEVENSON

Made in the USA
Middletown, DE
11 April 2025

74036744R10119